Focus on Features

Life-like Portrayals in Appliqué

Charlotte Warr Andersen

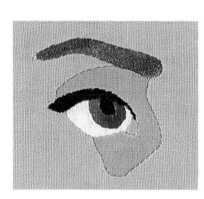

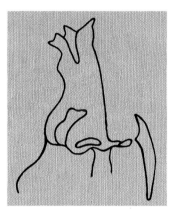

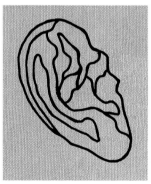

 C&T PUBLISHING

Copyright © 1998 Charlotte Warr Andersen

Developmental Editor: Barbara Konzak Kuhn
Technical Editor: Cyndy Lyle Rymer
Book Design: Bobbi Sloan
Cover Design: Micaela Carr; details of *The Wrangler, Kurt Browning, Fair as Flowers,*
and *Scruffy* shown on front cover.
Electronic illustrations by Christina Jarumay, Jay Richards, and Aubry Andersen,
©C&T Publishing, Inc.
All photography courtesy the individual artists unless otherwise noted.

Library of Congress Cataloging-in-Publication Data

Andersen, Charlotte Warr
    Focus on Features: life-like portrayals in appliqué / Charlotte Warr Andersen.
        p.   cm.
    Includes bibliographical references and index.
    ISBN 1-57120-053-3 (papertrade)
        1. Appliqué. 2. Face in art. 3. Quilting.   I. Title.
TT779.A523   1998
746.46'041—dc21   98-3694
                                                                         CIP

Published by C&T Publishing, Inc.
P.O. Box 1456
Lafayette, California 94549

Printed in Hong Kong
10 9 8 7 6 5 4 3 2 1

Dear Reader, Crafter, & Artist,

All of life is based upon the fact that there are always things left unsaid; better, more efficient and creative ways of doing things occur; and technology changes the way things can be done. So *Focus on Features* contains ways of improving upon the methods that I have taught.

The actual drawing process of Appliqué for Realism is the main emphasis of this book. Even though what I do is essentially tracing from a photograph, there are still variables that make even tracing seem intimidating. People tell me, "Oh, you have to be an artist to do that!" Maybe you do have to have an eye for this drawing process. But I do believe it is something that can be taught and learned—it just takes the true desire to learn it. Each time I've instructed students in the process of Appliqué for Realism in workshop after workshop, I am better able to describe the actual train of thought that comes while tracing from a photograph—why I draw the line where I draw it, why that line becomes the shape it does, why these multiple shapes fit together to make the proper visual image, and why shading works the way it does.

In class I usually project a picture of some hunky movie star and trace a line drawing from the photograph for the students to see that actual process. I think it is the most instructive part of the workshop and it helps immensely to watch as I point out each shape that is drawn. Here, I have tried to put that demonstration into book form.

With enough thought and attention, anyone can create a reasonable pictorial drawing from a photograph. You just need to know the principles and theories that go into this creative process. As with everything in our existence, there are rules that tell us what to do. During your early education, you have learned how to spell by using the rules that dictate word construction and phonetics. Once you learned to spell, you were rewarded by being able to read. It is good and needful to learn rules, but after learning them you also know when it's appropriate to break the rules that can be broken.

I feel the same way about this book as the statement Angela Gair makes about her book, *Tonal Values*: "Writing an art [quilt] instruction book is always a hazardous venture because, in attempting to explain the principles involved in painting [quilting], it is difficult to avoid giving the impression that there is a

Tracing a photograph on a lightbox.

right way and a wrong way to do things...Every compositional "rule" can be broken—and has been on many occasions. What I am attempting to do here is to offer some starting points from which to set off on your own chosen path toward the expression of your ideas."

Learn what you can and take that which will be beneficial to you and use it. The knowledge that we thought useless may pop back out of your head in a future time of need. Everything we have learned during our lives can come into play during the creative process. Believe it or not, reading, science, and math all provide enrichment for our artistic endeavors and examples can be seen at every quilt show.

With *Focus on Features,* I will also show more examples of the reverse layering technique. Because it might be a tricky concept to grasp, I think showing a few more step-by-step projects will be of service. Also, I have been exploring the possibilities of incorporating my reverse layering techniques with machine work. I know quilters who abhor the slowness of hand appliqué. There are means of appliquéing with a satin stitch (cover stitch) which gives agreeable results. Blind-hem stitch appliqué is also a possibility if the pattern or design is not too complicated. So, prepare to delve into the realm of pictorial appliqué once again.

Completed portrait of Eskild Andersen

Let's Review

A few changes have taken place in the availability of some equipment and supplies that I would like to inform you of, and a review of the Appliqué for Realism technique will refresh what you learned from the first book, *Faces & Places*.

THE SUBJECT— THE CHOICE IS ALL YOURS

Selecting a subject is the first step in starting a project. If you think that you have no artistic skill at drawing or even if you can draw, I feel that you can achieve the most desirable results if you work from a picture or photograph. In choosing a photograph, you may want to consider a few things:

Professional and Amateur Photography

Any photograph can be made to work with this process, but an unremarkable photograph takes greater artistic skill to be translated into a fabric collage that is shaded and dimensional. You may have a snapshot of a loved one in your collection that reaches out and tickles your heart strings. Perhaps the expression on the face is appealing, or the pose or angle of the body intriguing, all of which can be translated into fabric and/or embroidery by simply tracing the figure. However, if you look appraisingly at this same photograph and see very little in the way of shadows, it will be hard to create a look of dimension without them. The figure will look flat and one-dimensional. Shadows can be added to an otherwise flat-looking photograph but it takes artistic skill and a bit of imagination.

Candid photographs that are taken on the spur of the moment with no planned lighting can range anywhere from abysmal to captivating as everyone can attest to after bringing home a roll of film from the developers. Sometimes posing seems like the better solution but then the spontaneity can be lost. A pro-fessional portrait photographer gets paid for well-lit and flattering portraits of his subjects. When students bring photographs to class that they have paid to have taken, I find very few of them that aren't useable for creating an illusion of dimension in fabric, especially if the photographer has cast lovely, soft shadows from the side. But as much as I admire professional photographs and the people who take them, I can't see running to one every time I want to create a quilt portrait. It can be quite expensive and I can't say I like sharing the glory of creation with the photographer. Though the photographs I take are quite mediocre as photographs go, I can still use them to create great quilts. My advice is this: if you don't have that terrific photograph right there, ready in hand and useable, take LOTS of photographs. That is what I have been doing for this book, using rolls and rolls of film. Most of the shots are not even worth looking at, but some are workable and I have even taken a few good or maybe great pictures—at least when it comes to their usefulness for translating into fabric appliqué.

Copyright

What is the purpose of your quilt and what do you intend to do with it? If you are making the quilt for your own enjoyment, to hang in your own house or to give as a gift to a friend or relative, you can make use of any picture, photograph, or artwork you choose for inspiration for your piece.

If you have taken the photograph you are using yourself, you don't have to worry about copyright at all since the photograph is your own copyrighted material. However, you will need to worry about infringing upon someone's copyright if you are using a photograph or artwork that was taken or cre-ated by someone other than yourself or a close fam-ily member, and you plan to make the quilt to enter a contest or a large quilt show, or if you would like it published in a book, magazine, or catalog, or if you intend to make a pattern for the quilt and sell it.

Pictures, photographs, sculpture, paintings, graphic arts and even advertisements are considered intellectual property and automatically have been copyrighted the moment they were created. Any creative undertaking, including a quilt, that is modeled substantially after an existing photograph or artwork is considered derivative art. Written permission will need to be obtained from the creator of the intellectual property before you can make any public or commercial use of a derivative quilt you intend to make.

Even photographs you have paid to have taken are most likely copyrighted. Say you had a picture taken of your son or daughter at a commercial photograph studio and paid handsomely to have well-done prints made in several sizes suitable for framing. Were you to decide you'd like to take one of those prints to a copy store, such as kinko's®, and ask to have them make you a transfer of one of those pictures to put on the front of a T-shirt, the copy store would refuse to do it. That is because the photography studio owns the copyright on those photographs and the copy store will be violating the rights to those photographs if they print it on your T-shirt. You have to have permission from the studio or photographer.

Ann Peterson decided to make a quilt based on a photograph she had to have taken of her daughter, Erin. Had she kept the quilt to herself to hang in her home for her own personal enjoyment, she would not have had to worry about getting permission from the photographer. However, she did decide to allow me to publish the quilt in this book. She asked for and received permission from the photographer who took the picture. She also used a separate painting for the background behind Erin. She asked for and was granted permission for use of that artwork in her quilt.

Girl with Umbrella, 1997, 60" x 73", Ann Gail Peterson, Davis, California (photo by David G. Peterson). Worked from a photograph taken by Frances Constantino with background inspired by a painting "Keukenhof Stream" by Kevin D. Miles & Wendy Schaefer-Miles. Ann loved the way her daughter, Erin, looked peeking out from under the umbrella.

Degree of Difficulty

Reverse layering has applications in all types of appliqué. You may choose to appliqué a whole person or just a face, or that of your pet, and even individual items like mountains or trees or the water contained within landscapes; all are candidates for this technique. Details can best be accomplished with reverse appliqué; if the piece has shadows and dimension, layering works best.

Look at the picture you have selected. What is the size of the quilt you intend to make? Smaller is not necessarily easier. Say if you are doing a face and it has a detailed eye in it, those details can only be accomplished in so small a size—more stitching may actually be involved in a larger piece but, the larger the shape, the easier it is to stitch. Ask yourself just how much of the picture you are using that you want to portray in fabric. The picture may contain a whole figure—you may just want to do the bust-type portrait. The

Lora, Blair and Julie, 1997, 84" x 84" Lora Kilver Lacey, The Woodlands, Texas, and Annette Walser Kilver, Jacksonville, Illinois (photo by Thomas Anastasion). Lora and her mother, Annette, looked through family photographs and agreed that this one, taken by Lora's grandfather at Christmastime, would be the perfect topic for a joint project. Lora stands in the middle with her siblings on either side.

background may be undesirable—you can plug in another background and combine two totally different pictures.

Lora Lacey and Annette Kilver created their quilt with three full figures in it—the quilt is seven feet square so they could accomplish this. The background they used was not in the photograph but derived from memory and imagination. How much of your chosen project do you think you can create with fabric and appliqué?

I feel that anything can be done in appliqué, you just need to think up a procedure for doing it. Special fabrics can create special effects, and embroidery can be added in places that can't be done otherwise.

Little to Big

If your picture is already the size you want to use, simply trace over it. However, if you have a snapshot and want to do a life-size portrayal, you will need to enlarge your photograph by some means. You can

have a photographic enlargement done from your snapshot, but this can be very expensive. You can have a copy store make a blow-up of your snapshot, but black and white photocopies tend to disintegrate and lose detail as they get larger. If you want to enlarge by photocopy, I would advise that you use a color photocopier as it retains the color and detail you need. Even if you are enlarging a black and white photograph I would still recommend a color photocopier—the results will be much more useable. A computer, scanner, and color printer can also be used to make enlargements. Scan the snapshot in, instruct the computer program what size you would like the photograph enlarged to, and it will print it out in sections which you then have to tape together.

All of the above mentioned methods of enlarging involve making a larger copy of the photograph itself. The disadvantage to using an enlarged photograph is that you then have to lay tracing paper over the top of that photograph. I have yet to find a tracing paper that does not obscure some of the details and shadings that I need to see. Tracing paper is also not suitable for an actual pattern—it is flimsy and will not hold up under the wear and tear. After drawing your pattern on the tracing paper you then have to duplicate it on a sturdier paper that will stand up to much handling.

My preferred method of enlarging the snapshot is to use one of three projectors: a slide projector, an overhead projector, or an opaque projector. Any of these three projectors will cast an enlarged image on a wall, which is steady and smooth. You can then move the projector forward or back to dictate the size the image is going to be. Once you have focused the projector to the desired size, you tape a sturdy but somewhat translucent piece of paper in place. The pattern is then drawn or traced from the projected image.

One handy new item that I have found is an opaque projector called the Tracer®. It is made by the Artograph Company and can be found at many craft and art stores. The Tracer is made mostly of plastic, can project from a photograph up to a 6" x 6" size (the instructions say you can project a larger-sized picture by moving the projector to different sections of the picture but I find this is far from accurate because portions cannot be properly aligned), and will enlarge from two to twenty times (though photographs get quite fuzzy much over ten times larger), and is very

Tracer Opaque projector

reasonably priced for retail at $75 to $80. The optics of the lens of this projector are surprisingly good and cast as sharp an image as its much pricier counterparts.

Norman Rockwell sometimes used a projected image to help create his paintings. In my readings I have discovered that techniques similar to this have been in use for centuries. Illustrations in the book *Geometry and the Visual Arts* by Dan Pedoe show etchings by Albrecht Dürer in which he visualizes devices for making true representations onto paper or canvas. One shows a frame divided into squares by means of black threads strung horizontally and vertically to create a grid. The frame was then placed between the subject and the artist and, using a fixed sight, the artist interprets what he sees square by square. Pedoe also reports of artists using what is called a camera obscura. "Leonardo Da Vinci…is the first writer to discuss this device, which is exactly like a pinhole camera, but without photographic film at the back."

I always find it intriguing to read of methods artists use to gain more accurate images, and feel it reassuring to know that "tracing" and like methods are well-used and acceptable techniques.

MAKING A PATTERN

Once all your preparations are done, your picture is selected and enlarged by whichever method you have chosen, it is time to begin drawing the pattern.

In Shape

The most important point you have to remember in this pattern-making process is that, even though I call it drawing, you are not drawing or sketching in the traditional sense. When using a pencil to create a portrait in the pencil medium, feathery lines are created, texture and shades are gently added with the point and sides of the pencil, and fine lines can be drawn anywhere they are desired. This method does not work for creating a pattern which will then be duplicated in fabric. For fabric, everything you draw has to become a shape because shapes are all that can be made out of fabric. When these shapes are sewn together they create lines—the seamline—so all the lines you draw as you are tracing from your photograph have to join end-to-end to create shapes.

If you think about a traditional quilt made of squares, triangles, rectangles, diamonds, etc., the elements that make up these quilts are all shapes, or complete and closed forms. These shapes all join together to make seamlines; the exception being the edge or border of the quilt. All the shapes have finite edges. A fabric portrait has to work the same way. Although the shapes are much more complicated and amoeba-like than a traditional quilt, they are still finite. If you draw a line where the end is just dangling, there is no shape that can be cut out of fabric for the line has not been joined end-to-end.

Dangling line

So when you draw or trace from a photograph, you have to remember that everything has to become a shape.

The three illustrations on the following page demonstrate the way appliqué patterns need to be drawn. The photograph is a picture of my nephew,

Ryan

Sketch of Ryan:
Do not draw a pattern like this.

Line Pattern of Ryan:
Your pattern should be bold, clear shapes.

Ryan Cox. The first drawing is a sketch, which will not be useable for appliqué. The second is a line drawing where every line connects to become a shape—this image can be appliquéd.

You may notice that as a drawing the one that is sketched is much more attractive. But we need to go beyond that sketch. Once the colors and values are applied to the shapes of the properly drawn line drawing we can get that sense of dimension that is readily seen in the first drawing.

CONSTRUCTION

Little has changed in the products, tools, and fabrics that I prefer to use for hand appliqué. Cotton fabrics are still the easiest to stitch, but I'll use almost any fabric as long as it gives the look I want. My markers must be non-chemical and removable. Scissors, pins, and needles—all of the best quality—are what I need to work with. I still use Fraycheck® for working in tiny corners that have a tendency to fray, and prefer it over other brands even though some of them claim they will not stain your fabric. I find the consistency of the liquid to be more controllable than the others. Instead of painting it on your fabric, you may want to consider purchasing a Tip Pen®, which is a tiny metal cap that you can fit onto your bottle of Fraycheck. The tip

helps to give you a fine, precise line of the liquid where you want it.

I have had one change of attitude about the thread I use. I have said I will use any thread, with no care as to the brand or quality, just as long as it matches the fabric. Lately, I have definitely leaned toward using 100% cotton machine-embroidery thread. It is fine, comes in many colors, and appliqué stitches made with this thread will almost disappear if the thread is at least a near match to the fabric color. It comes in two brands that I know of: Mettler, a 60 weight thread (don't use the 30 weight since it's too thick for hand appliqué) that many quilt shops carry, and DMC®, a 50 weight thread that may be slightly harder to find but comes in 196 solid colors.

As I mentioned in the Introduction, I have also come up with a way to construct faces, figures, or other subjects on the sewing machine. This method also utilizes the cotton machine-embroidery thread and a product called Threadfuse™. Look for this technique in the last chapter (page 78).

But before we can get into fabric and construction, we must have that all-important pattern first. And to do something original you will want to be able to trace and draw from your own photograph. So in the upcoming chapter I'll discuss light and form, two of the basic elements of making pictorial representations.

Fair as Flowers, 1997, 36" x 39", Hui-Yen Lin, Kaohsiung, Taiwan (photo by Chen Gim). This is a lovely self-portrait of the artist derived from a photograph. A plethora of hand appliquéd roses surround her.

Our Lady of the Sierra, 1996, 60" x 96", Carol Spalding, Oakhurst, California (photo by Heidi Vetter). This quilt was designed and made for the new Catholic Church in Oakhurst. The Church's name is also "Our Lady of the Sierra." Carol also depicts local wildlife and vegetation in this quilt.

Shedding Light on the Subject

"Among the studies of natural causes and reasons Light chiefly delights the beholder."
— *Leonardo Da Vinci*

Kurt Browning, 1995, 36" x 42", Avril Bright, Ottawa, Ontario, Canada (photo by Chris Kravit). One of the most reknown figure skaters of our time, this portrait of Browning is skillfully derived from a photograph by Dino Ricci. The sense of light and shadow is remarkable. Avril thinks he is a marvelous example of the skater becoming the music.

LOOKING FOR THE LIGHT

It may not seem so, but of little importance among why we need light is that we require light to make our eyes work. Certainly we could live without sight, but vision makes our lives so much easier and more pleasurable. Light forms all visual aspects of our world—it's what gives us vision. Without sight, or if we all lived in darkness, it would be difficult to create paintings, sculpture, and, of course, quilts that are representational depictions of the world around us. And, if none of us could see, there would be no purpose in creating visual art. Quilts would still be useful for their utilitarian aspects—we would still need their warmth and tactile feel—but there would be no purpose in making them look pretty or colorful.

Those who wish to create realistic looking art need to make careful observations of light and its functions, for light visually defines our world for us. As light plays across the surfaces, contours, and structures that surround us, we can see the shape and form of those objects. Depending on the object, as the light strikes it we see opacity (light does not pass through the object), translucency (some light passes through the object), and/or transparency (most or all of the light passes through the object). As the direction the light is coming from changes, the objects we see change with each new angle—some parts are lit, other parts are in the dark; shadows are cast the opposite direction the light is coming from.

When it comes to the effects of light, our moon is one of the simplest forms in nature that we can easily observe—a globe or sphere. With the weather cooperating, we can step outside and see how light plays upon the moon's surface and watch during its twenty-nine day cycle the changes it goes through:

Moon phases

learned sitting in those higher math classes. But when it came to geometry something clicked a little bit. I was not so totally lost as I was in the other classes. Perhaps it was because we were again working with forms that related to the real world—circles, spheres, squares, rectangles, triangles, arcs, lines, planes, intersections—these were shapes my brain could picture.

Now, in mentioning geometry, I am not expecting you to do anything the least bit complicated with it.

"The moon shows progressively different phases as it moves along its orbit around the earth. Half the moon is always in sunlight, just as half the earth has day while the other half has night. The phases of the moon depend on how much of the sunlit half can be seen at any one time. In the phase called the new moon, the face is completely in shadow. About a week later, the moon is in the first quarter, resembling a luminous half-circle; another week later, the full moon shows its fully lighted surface; a week afterward, in its last quarter, the moon appears as a half-circle again."[1]

In between the above-mentioned phases we can see sunlit portions of the moon in various shapes—sickle moon, gibbous moon—it changes as it waxes and wanes. What portion of light and darkness we see depends on the direction the sun's light is coming from. This simple observation can be applied to the drawing and tracing of our patterns. All solid objects we look at are made of masses and geometric forms and light helps us determine the shape of each object.

SIMPLE GEOMETRY

Oh, no! I've mentioned one of the dreaded words. Yes, we are using geometry here but only in its most primitive forms. Most of us cringe at the mere thought of higher math. Usually I did abysmally in algebra and now I recall next to nothing of what I

[1]*Funk & Wagnall's New Encyclopedia.*
New York: R. R. Donnely & Sons, 1990.

Geometric shapes

We are not going to even consider formulas, postulates, or theorems. I only want you to think about the visual shapes, surfaces, and solids that are the very basic elements of geometry.

Ted Seth Jacobs says in his book, *Light for the Artist,* "Geometric forms are useful because they are simple and uncomplicated. They clearly show the actions of light. From the study of light effects on simple forms, we learn the action of light in very complex situations."

Figures, faces, and animals are not what we traditionally look at as being geometric forms—we usually think of shapes that have rigid symmetry when we think of geometry. But as we break down the structure of something as complicated as, say, a face, we can start to identify the basic forms that combine to make up the complex planes of facial features, and figure out how light plays across these forms by the angle of the light.

Also from Jacobs: "To avoid possible misunderstandings, let me clearly state that no one's head is shaped like an egg. Nor is the human body like some sort of doll, made out of jointed, egg-shaped sections. Nor is it made of spheres, rectangles, or any other geometric shapes. The head is shaped like a head and the body like a body. And yet, and yet, beneath the subtle and complex shapes of the body there seem to lie simpler forms. These underlying basic forms give to the surface of the body a fullness, an amplitude."

I have already discussed what occurs when light hits a sphere—the cycles of the moon. Picture what happens to other geometric forms with light falling upon them.

We can relate some of these shapes or half-shapes to body parts: an upper arm is barrel-like in shape, a foot like a wedge, a nose is somewhat like half a cone, eyeballs are spheres within our heads and eyelids take on the shape of the portion of the

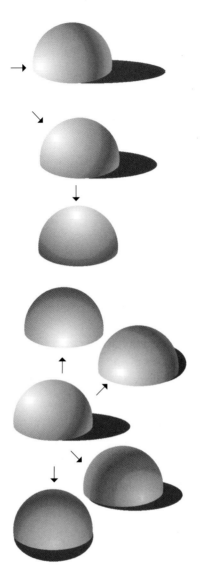

Dome (convex) in plain.
Arrows indicate angle of light.

sphere they cover, a finger is stacked like two barrels with an elongated dome on the top, whereas a thumb is only one barrel with an elongated dome on top. Look at yourself in a mirror, use a bit of imagination, and see if you can pick out geometric shapes or portions of those shapes that relate to different parts of your anatomy.

"OUTS" AND "INS"

Now it is time to discuss "outs" and "ins" or what can also be called positive space and negative space. These are very important considerations when you are looking at light. The simplest way I can describe "outs" and "ins" is with the following analogy. First, close your eyes and use your imagination. You have a vast plain (or plane in the geometric sense) before you. The land is flat and extends every which way you look, except in one direction there is a lone mountain standing before you. That mountain is definitely an "out." It protrudes into the air above the plain. Now picture walking across that flat plain and you come to a hole in the earth. It could be a crater where a large meteor has taken a chunk out of the land, or it could be a quarry where rock is being unearthed. Whether crater or quarry it is definitely an "in." For the purposes of exploring light we will think of "outs" as positive space and "ins" as negative space.

Now let's look at how light affects "outs" and "ins." Whatever the direction of the light source, only so much of a three-dimensional shape can be lit; the unlit part of the shape falls into shadow. For illustrative purposes, I will use the example of a dome (half a sphere) in the middle of a plain (plane). Observe how the dome changes according to the direction from which the light is coming.

The arrow indicates the angle of light. When the light is coming from low on one side, close to the horizon, only one side of the dome is lit and a shadow is cast in the opposite direction. Bring the light source up a little higher and more of the dome is lit; the shadow becomes shorter. If the light source is directed from straight above the dome (what could be considered high noon) the dome is fully lit and there are no shadows. And, in the last two steps, the reverse of the first two steps occur—the opposite side of the dome is lit and the shadow falls in the opposite direction. Because the dome protrudes above the surface it is positive space, where light falls upon it and it casts shadows outside its own shape.

There are two types of shadows: form shadows and cast shadows. Form shadows are the dark values that are on the surface of the shape that is being observed. Cast shadows are made by the form blocking the light from falling on surfaces in the opposite direction of the angle of light. Form shadows usually have soft edges that taper from light to dark, whereas cast shadows usually have much crisper edges. Changes also occur when the light revolves around the object as well as passing overhead.

The best actual examples I could find of this "in" and "out" dome on the plain that I'm trying to explain is my microwave muffin pan. Notice cast shadows and form shadows.

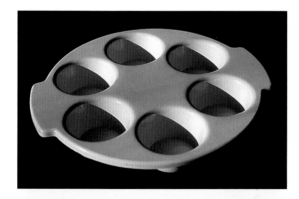

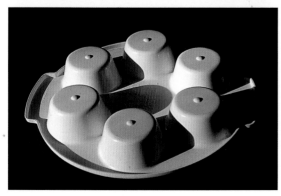

Muffin pan

Backlighting creates a challenging situation with many form and cast shadows. Here is a portrait I stitched from a photo of my daughter, Aubry, which was backlit. I think I have aged her a lot in this portrayal and perhaps when she is 30 she'll look like this.

You may be wondering why I'm making you look at all these geometric shapes when what you want to draw is a face, figure, building, tree, animal—something real anyway. I want you to observe these shapes as they look in light and shadow because there are similar shapes within the structure of all of those mentioned above.

NATURAL VS. ARTIFICIAL LIGHT

Shapes and figures look different in natural light than they do in artificial light and there are all sorts of variables in both types of light. Since I have decided to use my own photographs in my own quilts for the most part, so I won't have to worry about infringing on someone's copyright, I have been taking photographs in a great variety of situations and have learned a bit about photography in the process.

I photographed several faces in various lighting situations. Let's examine the ones done in natural light first. Most of the photographs that I had taken during the peak daylight hours on bright, sunny days I do not care for. The sun is harsh and glaring, making the light and shadows too distinct. Overhead angles of light are not necessarily flattering to faces either. Sunlight can be tricky to work with also.

Dallin DeWitt

Nathan Merkley

Dylan Andersen

I took this picture of Dallin about 5 o'clock on an August afternoon. I thought the sun had softened enough but it was still quite strong and Dallin couldn't face into the light without closing his eyes. I also did not notice that a nearby chain-link fence was casting strange little shadows across his figure.

In the photo of Nathan Merkley, I was under a tree and you can see that there are weird shadows all over his face.

My son Dylan has his hat on so his face is mostly in shadow with a harsh wedge of sunlight coming across his right cheek, but also notice that there must be a source of reflected light coming from his left. The left side of his face is lighter than the center and the darkest value is running down the middle of his nose.

The photos of my in-laws, Karen and Peder Andersen, were taken outside in the early afternoon on a very overcast day. These pictures are relatively flat and have no dramatic shadows. They would be useful for making fairly simple likenesses of people with a lot of wrinkles and contours in their faces.

My favorite time of day for taking photographs is close to sunset. Sometimes this time of day is called "the golden hour." Sunlight is usually a bit softer then. I remember being at a school folk-arts festival that was held after school hours on the commons ground. The junior high school my son attends is ethnically diverse and the different students were performing the native dances of their ancestral backgrounds—Navajo, African, Polynesian, Scandinavian, etc. It was this "golden hour" of day and everyone looked so beautiful and I was just dying because I had forgot to bring my camera.

Karen Andersen

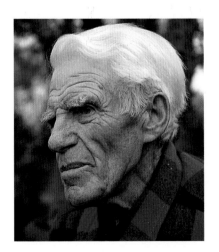

Peder Andersen

I took these pictures of Gladys White and her friend, Renelle Acres (both members of the Fraser Valley Quilt Guild) about an hour before sunset in White Rock, Vancouver, B.C. The sky was just slightly overcast and the light was soft. They still had to squint a little when they looked toward the sun, but all the pictures I took of them turned out beautifully.

Gladys White

Renelle Acres

Judy Cox

Eskild Andersen

Peder Andersen

My sister, Judy Cox, looks golden in this photograph. The sun was right on the horizon and about to go down when I snapped this picture. Even though, theoretically, this is the right time of day, this photograph is too strongly lit for my liking.

Perhaps five minutes later, I took this photo of my husband, Eskild, in close to the same spot. Much of the light has left the scene, but I can still get a good sense of light and shadow on him and I can easily make out all portions of his face.

I have found that, in some ways, I can be more successful with artificial light and setting up my own situations. I seldom use the flash on my camera—I don't like the stark way it lights up the contours of a face and it doesn't produce the desirable shadows as in the photograph of my father-in-law, Peder Andersen. There are exceptions for flash photographs; some can be made to work.

Butterfly Man, 1995, 37" x 41", Heather Rose, Flagstaff Hill, South Australia (photo by Grant Hancock). This quilt is worked from photos Heather took of her son, Derek. He had grown a beard and Heather added the tatoos for a bit of fun. She says, "I wanted to show two images of man. Tough and volatile, ready to take on anything; soft and voluble with yielding emotions." Heather created *Butterfly Man* from a flash photograph she took of her son. It is a wonderful quilt and you can really sense the fullness and dimension of him.

Peder Andersen	Peder Andersen	Rohana Liyanage

You do not need fancy professional lighting equipment to take good photographs indoors with artificial light. These pictures of my father-in-law were taken in an unlit room during daylight with a desk lamp with a forty-watt bulb shining on his face. I used 400 speed film, which of course helps to capture more light. (He looks somewhat like Spencer Tracy, doesn't he?) I love these pictures and intend to stitch them up soon. The bluish sections on the back of his head comes from window light. I will appliqué only the lighted parts of his face and the blue backlight, and let the rest fall to a black background.

For the photograph of Rohana Liyanage, I used two desk lamps coming from the same direction. Both had sixty-watt bulbs and having more light meant that I could see all of his face. I used the 400 speed film again. It made for an attractive lighting situation. For both of these indoor settings I used regular slide film and these everyday, ordinary tungsten light bulbs. The flesh tones in these photographs look golden because

tungsten bulbs cast a yellow light. I think it is an attractive coloration but if this bothers you it can be corrected. If you are using print film, simply tell the store doing the developing that incandescent lights were used and they can make a color correction when they are developing your film. Slide film cannot be color corrected but you can buy a tungsten film at professional photography stores that will compensate for yellow light.

Fluorescent lights cast a green light as you can see in the photographs of the hands.

I do not find this coloration attractive and have found out that I do not want to use fluorescent light in my photographs. Print film can also be color corrected for this problem—just tell them that the photographs were taken under fluorescent lights.

I hope this short overview of photography is helpful. Again, my best advice is that when you are taking your own photographs, take lots of them so you have a wide variety to pick from. Hopefully one will work for you.

ONWARD

This whole process of drawing a pattern is a combination of tracing what I actually see in the photograph, drawing what I think or believe to be there (artistic license), paying attention to the undulations of differing contours, and stylizing the shapes and color values I see so that I will be able to appliqué them. It all combines into a line drawing that is simple yet descriptive, similar to a paint-by-number canvas, and something which a quilter will be able to interpret in fabric.

"You are made like your quilts," he said softly ... *"Strange geometrical hinges."*—from the novel *Hearts and Bones* by Margaret Lawrence.

Face to Face

DETERMINING THE ANGLE OF LIGHT

If I were an obsessive person, every time I took a picture I would write down and record the angle of light for that picture. Knowing the exact angle the light is coming from will help me in determining the way the light is hitting different shapes and forms within a face or figure, and I will be able to draw my shapes more correctly. However, I do not feel compelled to do this and I am not organized enough to keep track of everything I should. I think that it is adequate to approximate the angle of light and there are always clues in a picture to help you figure that out.

One of the first things you should do when you look at a photograph that you want to duplicate in fabric is determine approximately where the light is coming from. For this appliqué process it is much easier if there is only one light source, but many times there may be more than one; in the sunlight there may be refracted light bouncing off some of the surroundings; indoors there may be light streaming in a window, plus one or several lamps or fixtures that are lit. You need to determine or at least guess what is the primary light source. If there are secondary light sources you can choose to ignore them or deal with them later.

You may want to draw an arrow on your photograph showing the direction you think the light is coming from. A photograph is a two-dimensional object so you need to think about this arrow in spatial terms as well. Imagine where the light is in rotation around the subject.

My Ian, 1996, 18" x 22", LaDonna Christensen, Los Osos, California (photo by Jeff Greene, Image West Photography). Working from a wistful picture of Ladonna's grandson, the quilt features an unusual portrait angle with Ian squinting into the sun and wind. The light source for this portrait is coming from the direction Ian is looking.

THE WRANGLER—BOB MELSON

Bob Melson is the Head Wrangler at the Nine Quarter Circle Guest Ranch in Gallatin Gateway, Montana. I have taught at several quilting retreats there and decided that Bob would make a great subject for an appliqué piece. When I asked for permission to take his picture, he consented (I think he likes having his picture taken because he knows he's cute and has a terrific Western face) and I took several shots of him both indoors and outdoors. I was lucky enough to have one come out to my liking. The lighting in the photograph is not as striking and bold as I would like it to be (the day was slightly overcast), but it has enough contrast that I can pick out lines and shapes that will re-create Bob's rugged good looks.

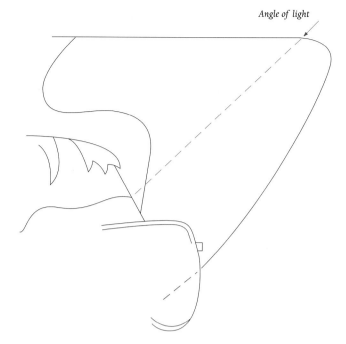

Line drawn from brim of hat to edge of cast shadow on brow shows angle of light.

Bob's face is turned away from me to the left. Since I did not record the angle the light was coming from at the time I took this picture, I need to take a guess at it. There are clues in the photograph to help me. The projection (profile) of his nose is the most lighted portion of the picture and the rest of the nose is mostly in shadow. By this, I know the light is coming somewhere from Bob's left. Most of his forehead is also in a shadow which is cast by the brim of his hat. If I were to draw an imaginary line from the edge of the shadow to the brim of his hat, this gives me approximately the angle the light is coming from.

(If we could see his cast shadow we could draw a line from the top of his shadow to the top of his head and that would also, and more accurately, show us the angle of light.) I then take a guess as to how far to his left the sun is and I picture in my head, spatially, the actual direction the light is coming from. This will help me determine which way to draw curves when I look at the different substructures of his face.

For starters, I trace over the easily seen parts of the picture — the outline of his face, hair, and hat, his sunglasses, the hairy shape of his mustache, the general outline of his clothing, and the details of his ear are quite apparent, as is the chin strap for his hat. If I

draw the things I can readily see first, it makes it easier to determine lines for the shadowy parts or the things that there aren't definite lines for. Then it is time to go on those parts where you have to do more thinking and figuring.

Let's consider flesh tones first. When I am doing a life-sized portrait, I usually try to keep my flesh tones within three to five different shades, gradations, or values. If I decide Bob is tan in color, I look for three to five shades of tan in values from light to dark—tan becomes brown in its darker values. I try to go for three to five shades because I don't usually like to chop up a face too much—it's not flattering and it gets too complicated. Another reason is because it's quite hard to find flesh tones in fabric. I ended up with seven shades of tan for Bob though. I seemed to need every line I had drawn and it helped to make him more rugged looking.

I usually ignore highlights in photographs. While they are important in paintings, they tend to be distracting when interpreted in fabric and stand out as blaring patches. They distract from other, more important elements of the face. Bob's nose (out) seems to be highlighted because it is so much brighter than the rest of his face. However, this highlight makes up most of his nose and separates his nose from the slightly darker color of his cheek behind. So I have drawn in this highlight because I think it is important and I designate it to be a different color than the rest of his flesh tones. It is my number one color or value.

Now I start looking for the next lightest skin tone or number two color or value. I look for areas of his face that have approximately that color. Much of Bob's nose is the next lightest color, including the flair of his nostril. All that we can see of his left cheek seems to be close to that color. There is an area on his right cheek that comes close so I have drawn an area that works with the flow of his face. Inside that area is a smile line. I have decided to ignore that line for now — it would be too difficult to appliqué — but if I decide I need it I can embroider or quilt a line for it. There is also an area of this next lightest color on his brow ridge (out) and on the bridge of his nose (out) betwixt the metal parts of his sunglasses. There is a deep shadow on the far side of his nose that is created by his eye socket (in). Most of Bob's forehead seems to be

Then there is the lower curve of his cheek. These darker areas become color number five.

Much of the darkness along his jawline is created by stubble or five o' clock shadow. Since the lower parts of his jaw and chin are darker than the number five shapes I have just drawn, they become number six. Then there is a quite dark shape that is created partly by the shadow of his chin strap and partly by an indentation (in) of his jawbone. This is color number seven—more shades than I really want to use but I do see them all there and don't want to eliminate any of them. I don't want to add any more either so any of the other shapes that I draw that are flesh toned need to be made of one of those seven shades.

Now I go to work on Bob's neck. The front of his neck is catching some light. I compare it to other sections of his face and decide that it's close to the same shade as his forehead, which is color number three. Most of his neck looks about the same color as areas that I have designated as color four so that is what it becomes. The area at the back of his neck is very dark and could be either color six or seven—I chose to make it six. His ear protrudes out from his head and seems to catch more light than its surrounding flesh tones. I decided to make his ear number four and the shadows within it five for the upper one and six for the lower.

I see variations of color and value in Bob's mustache, so I decide to break it up into three different fabrics, but I can't see much variation in his hair so that is all of one color. It is very difficult to distinguish a line between his hair and his hat, but I want to differentiate between them with separate fabrics so I draw a line I think will work. I look for variations of value in his hat—it all looks black, but possibly you know by fabric-purchasing experience that there are many different blacks on the shelf and the variations will add dimension.

For the clothing I try to separate different entities—I see bandana, shirt, T-shirt underneath, vest and plaid jacket (lining is different) plus the scarf holder. For each of these items I will use two to four shades of colors that will make them look like separate pieces of his clothing. I draw in wrinkles, draping, and shadows.

I only want to portray head and shoulders so I try to lop the rest of his body in a pleasing fashion and plan to extend the points of the bandana into the border of the quilt.

lighter than the remaining parts of his face, so, even though it's a shadow, it becomes color or value number three.

As I am drawing these shapes I try to think about the contours of the face that influence the shape these lines should be drawn. For example, there is a slight dip in the line that separates the shadow on his forehead from his brow ridge (out) because there is an actual declivity (in) in the bone structure above the nose. There is a wrinkle (in) on his forehead that shows you how it dips—notice how that wrinkle line wavers—but I did not use this wrinkle line to draw my shape because that is not where I saw the value change.

Now I decide where I see the next value of tan. Most of the side of his face that is towards us is this next shade (color number four) but I am also looking for the next shade at the same time. Most of the lines for this number four shape are drawn with the curves radiating from the high point of that rounded cheek. There is a darker shape just above the ear piece of his sunglasses that is part wrinkle (in), partly the depression (in) of his temple. There is the line for the shadow that his sunglasses are casting on his face and within that shadow is a darker one that is the crease of his eye—this little crease I do want.

Now, for Bob's sunglasses, I could opt to do something easy and just make the lenses all one piece of fabric. But I have decided that I can see through the lenses of his sunglasses in the photograph and I want to achieve that look. So I draw what I can see—his right eye under the right lens and under the left lens, his left eye, eyelid, cheek, hat, and background.

You may be wondering why I would want to put myself to so much trouble and work. But I like giving myself these challenges and will explain how this look is accomplished in the Details section (page 72).

ALLYSSA

Allyssa Merkley is my niece's daughter and an adorable little girl. I was at a family gathering taking pictures of everyone in sight who was willing to let me. Allyssa did not want me to take her picture at first, as she doesn't know me very well and didn't really trust me. However, she saw everyone else getting their picture taken including the other kids around her age, so she finally relented. I think the suspicion is still quite apparent in her eyes in this picture.

This photograph was taken with my flash on so the angle of light in this picture is coming directly from my camera. In other words, it's coming straight from the front. I usually do not like flash photography for use in fabric portraits but there are exceptions. The flash works like a strobe that lights up everything very brightly—there are very few shadows on the subjects of the photograph, but there are almost always shadows cast behind them. The flash also can light up every little variation in hue in a face. These are very subtle variations but they can get distractive. You need to be selective about what you choose to use and what you choose to ignore with this type of photograph, more than with subtly lit photographs.

I believe that in certain cases flash photographs work better for portraits of children than it does for adults. Children have young, smooth faces that are rounder and lack the angles that older faces have. You want to keep your line drawing of them fairly simple because if you break their faces up too much, putting in too many shades and values, it tends to age them far past their years. For young children I would recommend that you use no more than three or four flesh tones for a face, maybe throwing in a fifth one if you absolutely have to.

I found this photograph of Allyssa appealing in its simplicity. I also wanted to see if that expression of mistrust would come across into my line drawing of her. When I did the drawings you see on the next pages, the photograph was projected so Allyssa's head is about six inches high from the top of her head to the bottom of her chin.

Children always seem to have such huge eyes, and this is where I start my drawing, tracing the eye white, iris, and pupil. I seldom worry about putting the highlight into the eyes, but sometimes I do draw it on the pattern in case I want to use it. I also include the tear duct at the corner of her eye. These all look much too small to appliqué but I will show you later that it can be done. Her eyelashes are very apparent and create a dark line above each eye. Her lower lashes only create a slight difference in shading in the photograph so I choose to ignore them for my portrait. I then trace the outline of her face, including the bit of ear that is showing and her little rosebud mouth with a line separating each lip. A delicate eyebrow shape is traced—this is on the bare edge of the size of a shape that I can reverse appliqué. Realistically, these eyebrows will probably end slightly larger when the actual appliqué is done but I will try to make them this small.

Allyssa has very fly-away hair, so I try to simplify it into something I can appliqué. To achieve that fly-away look I will have to do quite a few dagger points but that is the way I choose to portray her hair rather

Allysa Merkley

Figure 1. All easily drawn lines in place

Figure 2. The result of looking at the picture too hard.

than embroider or by thread painting. I then look for the highlights in her hair and designate a shape for each of those, and then I see that there are about two other shades in her hair—her main color and darker shadowed parts. The lines in Figure 1 are readily seen and don't require too much decision-making.

I then go back to do the shading in her face. If I look for every change of color, tone, or value that I see in her face, it doesn't work. The face gets chopped up too much and becomes rather scary looking and not at all flattering, as in Figure 2. I have decided I only want to use three values of flesh tones on Allyssa. One, the lightest color, for the main part of her face, then I look for distinct shadows, and decide if they are my number two value, or my number three value. If I choose my lines and shapes judiciously, I come up with the following drawing, Figure 3.

Here are some other places I could make less than flattering portrayals: There are shadows on either side of the bridge of her nose and under her eyebrows where the eye socket goes back into the head. Everyone has recessed areas under their eyes—they are what can be called "bags" when they show up more than we want them to—but everyone has these because it is the way the human face is structured. Allyssa has "bags" under her eyes—you can

see a difference in shading in that area. But if I draw them the way I see them and plug one of my darker flesh tones into that shape, it will really age Allyssa, as in Figure 4. She will no longer look like the twenty-one-month-old she is in the photograph. So I have drawn a shape that just barely hints at an indentation under her right eye and essentially ignored the one under her left eye, as you will see back in Figure 3.

Noses can be difficult—especially when the shapes are as fine as they are in Allyssa's face. If I go only by color, her nose looks pinker and darker than the surrounding flesh tones. If I isolate her nose and designate it as a darker pink color it means that I then need to appliqué it on top of the other flesh tones. It will not blend well with her face and could look more like a clown-nose, as in Figure 5.

In Figure 3, I chose to ignore the color change on her nose and just drew the areas that looked darker. I drew a shape that defines the undulations of the tip of her nose, which lets the upper part of the nose merge with the rest of her face. I cannot see her nostrils—there are actually highlights where you think her nostrils should be—so I don't worry about them. I think the shape I have drawn is descriptive enough for her nose and looks dainty and child-like.

Figure 3. Reasonable likeness, very doable.

Figure 4. Bags under her eyes make her look haggard.

Continuing with a description of Figure 3, there is a small dimple at the left corner of her mouth (I can't see one at the opposite corner). But I can see a slight shadow that will help give shape to her right cheek. This shadow continues under her mouth to show the recession between her mouth and chin. I round the line to give the proper shape to her chin. There are shadows that run up either side of Allyssa's face where her face curves back and the light of the flash is not hitting so directly. On the right side I choose to join this shadow with the lines I have drawn around her mouth and chin, and shape that line around the contours of her eye and temple. The shadow of the left side is drawn with a slight indentation to show a bit of hollow under her cheekbone.

After I have drawn in all these shadows I decide whether each will be a number two or a number three flesh tone and I number all my shapes accordingly. I draw her neck and a portion of her sweatshirt and my drawing is finished. I think the drawing of Figure 3 looks very much like Allyssa, since it is not too complicated and that look of suspicion is still in her eyes. Alright!

Figure 5. Drawing a nose like this makes her look clownish.

Mary Warr

MOM

For this photograph of my mother, Mary Warr, I set up the shot so the angle of light was coming from the side. It has the direction and intensity I most like to work with. I had her sit just inside my open front door which faces east. The time of day was early-afternoon so the sunlight was not coming through the door directly, but was diffused and pleasant. I put a black drape behind her so her gray hair would show up nicely.

Mom looks great at the age of eighty-two. Though she has wrinkles, most are not deeply carved into her face and rest lightly on her skin surface. If I choose to portray those light wrinkles at all, I will probably quilt them into the portrait rather than shade them with appliqué.

This photograph turned out relatively easy to trace since I had set up the shot the way I wanted it. I start with her eyes as I do for most portraits, tracing whites, irises, and pupils. The dark area that is part eyelashes, part shadow, hooks around and comes under the outer corners of her eyes so I draw them that way. I draw in the eyebrows, her nostrils—both of which are quite visible — and her lips. Then I trace the outline of her face, hair, neck, and clothing. Now it is time to look for the shade variations within these outlines. For the most part, in Allyssa's face (page 25), I decided which area of her face would be which value while I was drawing the shape. That is what worked best for her uncomplicated face and I was only using three flesh tones. My mother's face is much more complicated and I know I will be using five or more flesh tones. While I will be keeping different values in mind while I am drawing shapes, I will decide what value each of these shapes will actually be after I have drawn all the lines.

Mom has deep creases on her face. There are two "worry lines" between her eyebrows. (You'd have those, too, if you raised six children and three grandchildren.) I draw them as very narrow shapes—again

at the edge of what I can reverse appliqué, but I will try. Mom is a happy person and her smile lines on either side of her mouth are deep. They curve outward from the flare of her nostril, back into the corner of her mouth and continue down into her chin area. On the right side of the mouth I include the indentation under her lip, another wrinkle at the bottom of her chin, and join it to the shadow that runs up the right side of her face. I decide to ignore a lot of the mottled look of her chin. There is a medium value shadow on her chin and I use this to wrap around the mound of her chin, draw a bump for that slight declivity, bring it up until it almost joins the smile line on the left side of her chin, and then drop it down into her neck area.

I can see medium values on her right forehead, one runs down her nose, a little one on her right cheek, and different areas around her eyes.

I shade her lips because there are value changes as the light falls across them. Instead of making each individual tooth, I decide to make the teeth as a wedge of white (or off-white) with a value change a little more than half-way across. The back corners of her mouth fall to a dark charcoal gray. I find three different values in her hair. Then I draw wavy lines in her hair to simulate the curliness of it.

I draw these shapes remembering that I don't want to make this too complicated with an excruciating number of small pieces. I can't help but have more small shapes than with other portraits because Mom is an older person and has many more lines in her face. So I draw shapes that seem important and ignore others that aren't. I choose to ignore many of the little mottled shadows on her forehead. I could go on and on with a description of the lines I drew for Mom's face. Please compare the line drawing to the photograph and see how some things were ignored, while others were simplified or stylized, all with the idea of having something that is not too tedious to actually work through but still is a decent portrait.

Mother & Her Sisters, 1996, 37" x 52", Avril Bright, Ottawa, Ontario, Canada (photo by Chris Kralik). The photos used to make this quilt were taken in 1923. All the people shown in the quilt are now deceased and this piece holds dear memories for Avril.

Nuclear Family, 1996, 28" x 36", Avril Bright, Ottawa, Ontario, Canada (photo by Chris Kralik). Based on a family photograph, Avril is the baby on her mother's lap.

Caitlin on the Couch, 1996, 30" x 40", Jean Carter, Raliegh, North Carolina, (photo by Ray Barbour). Caitlin is Jean's beloved goddaughter and she made this portrait based on a photograph taken by the girl's mother.

Jaquelin Holzman, 1995, 20" x 24", Avril Bright, Ottawa, Ontario, Canada (photo by Rosemary Kralik). This woman is the current mayor of Ottawa and the fabric portrait is one in a series on famous Jewish people. It is worked from a photograph by John Rutherford.

View from a Seine Skiff, 1997, 42" x 33", Carol B. Kandoll, Petersburg, Alaska (photo by Thomas Anastasion). Carol lives in a small community on an island in the Inside Passage of Alaska surrounded by gorgeous scenery — the mountains she portrays are seen from the town. She made this quilt as a graduation present for her nephew to remind him of the beauty of home. The quilt hung at the local quilt show and everyone recognized the person in the quilt as Carol's nephew.

Grampy was a Sailor and So was His Father, 1996, 36" x 48" Heather Rose, Flagstaff Hill, South Australia (photo by Grant Hancock). Based on imagination and old family photos this quilt relates the history of Richard Murch, Heather's great grandfather, who sailed to the Boxer Rebellion in China in August of 1900. As well as the hand appliquéd figure, the quilt incorporates photos transfered to fabric.

CHAPTER FOUR

The Feature Story

"It is rather easy to draw what one expects to see, and this may differ from what the eye actually sees."
—Dan Pedoe, *Geometry and the Visual Arts*

Teddy, 1996, 26" x 31", Patricia K. Drennan, Albuquerque, New Mexico (photo by Pat Berrett). A moving portrait of Pat's youngest son, Teddy, who died in 1993 at the age of 26. Teddy was a policeman and Pat worked from his official photograph, but she hopes the sensitivity and softness that she always saw in him is apparent in this quilt.

And of course, the truer to shape the lines are drawn and the more impeccably they are worked into fabric, the more recognizable the individual will be.

EYES

Eyes are the most compelling feature of a face. They are what you want to see first when you look at a portrait. A recent issue of a news magazine featured a picture of Saddam Hussein on the cover. His face alone filled up the entire cover and a small figure of President Clinton was standing in front of Saddam covering his nose and mouth. The only thing really showing and the only thing you really noticed at first glance was Saddam Hussein's eyes, and, without reading any of the text on the cover, you knew exactly whose eyes those were.

Eyes can be simplified if you don't want to do tiny details. This drawing shows a simplified eye, one descriptive shape, and this is basically the type of eye I would make before I had discovered it wasn't all that much more work to do a detailed eye with eyebrow, lashes (done as one narrow strip), whites, iris, and pupil and, sometimes, the tiny pink tear duct at the corner of the eye.

Sometimes it seems like I have worked out all of this drawing process into formulas—an eye gets drawn a certain way with so many pieces; a mouth has two lips, is smiling or unsmiling; noses and ears have few variations. To a certain extent this is true but there are always variables in each and every face and figure. We all have essentially the same features—it's those subtle variations in shape and the way the features are combined that turn us all into individuals.

Simple one-piece eye shape with eyebrow

Stylized eye with all needed details

That is my formula for drawing an eye. It is a stylized eye but variables turn this formula into individual eyes. Some of these variables include: the actual shape of the eye; the shadows surrounding the eye; the fold in the eyelid. Also is it wide open? Is it squinting? Is it looking right or left, up or down, or is it a side view or angle other than a frontal view?

Variables in Individual Elements

Eyebrows: slender or bushy, covered by bangs, unibrow (like Frieda Kahlo), are they really that visible—some children have such pale eyebrows you can't see them. Lashes: Long and feathery (I usually make one even line, not making all those fine points it would take to make a feathery line), upper and lower lashes (I usually ignore lower lashes unless I can really see them or I want the person to look sexy and glamourous). Whites and Irises: Shape is the biggest variable here with the option of putting the little pink tear duct in, and placement of the iris along with choice of eye color. Pupil: Dilation.

NOSES

The human nose comes in all sorts of shapes and sizes. It seems to be the facial feature most of us worry about, probably because it is so prominent—sticking out there in front of everything else. I also think it's the hardest part of a portrait to draw because of that prominence. A nose seems to catch more light, cast shadows, and creates impossible shapes to appliqué, more so than any other feature of the face. From certain angles it overlaps other parts of the face and throws off the layering order. There can be places where a very thin line is all that shows the curvature and that line has to be widened so one can appliqué it. Shadows drawn the wrong way can make a nose look asymmetrical. If one is too heavy-handed with the shapes, a nose can become huge.

I do not have a formula for drawing a nose and I have to admit that sometimes I take a lot of artistic license with what I see. I do try to carefully observe

Treasure, 1997, 43" x 21", Barbara E. Friedman, San Diego, California (photo By Color Craft Company). Barbara was struck by the pensiveness of the photo of her cousin, Wendy Lynn Ora, and was inspired to make this quilt. Many fabrics were auditioned to capture this emotion and the eyes are very expressive of it. She seems to be watching from wherever she is, reminding us to treasure the time that we have and the people in our lives.

the shadows formed around a nose and work with them and manipulate them until I make shapes that seem to work. This is probably the area I use my eraser the most. If the nose doesn't look the way you want it to after you draw it, try rearranging your shapes a bit until you are satisfied.

Here are a few hints: Ignore any small bright highlights on the bridge or tip of the nose. Unless the light is coming from below chin level, there is almost always some sort of shadow under the nose. Draw narrow shapes to show the curl around the flare of the nostrils. Make the nose as simple as the shadows you see will allow.

Nixon, 1972, 18" x 23", Margaret Cusack, Brooklyn, New York (photo by Margaret Cusack). This portrait shows Margaret's ability to interpret faces in fabric (placed here because of the man's memorable nose).

MOUTHS

I do tend to stylize mouths. Here's a rule I think you can relate to—the wider open a mouth is the more complicated it gets. For most of the portraits I have done, I have opted for a closed mouth. I like a nice little Mona Lisa smile on the faces I make—it's simple and pleasing. But don't let a big, toothy grin stop

you. Just remember it's more work and it needs to be done right. I remember seeing a quilt years ago that had several beautiful portraits that were well-worked in hand appliqué. Everything looked great except for the portraits where the person was smiling. The artist, after having made the rest of the face including the lips, had satin stitched large, white teeth on top of the lips. Those teeth looked like gum glued to the lips. This is not the right way to accomplish it. Lips can be appliquéd on top of the face, but I prefer to reverse appliqué all parts of the mouth into the face as they are layered in real life. So as you are drawing mouths, keep in mind the order you will be appliquéing each piece and it will direct how you trace each shape.

Because light comes from overhead most of the time, the upper lip of a mouth will be darker than the lower lip. If the light is coming from the side, there may be two or three shades of lip color across a single lip. It's up to you if you want to do the work that this would take, but a face can look adequate with a single color on each lip. Many times when I draw men, I do not draw a separate lower lip. Instead I emphasize the shadow that is under the lip where the chin indents, and make the lower lip the same color as the lighter, surrounding flesh tones. I think this makes for a very masculine look (see photo at left).

In most cases, there will be some sort of indentation at each corner of the mouth, especially if the person is smiling. (The muscles in our faces pull the corners of the mouth under our cheeks.) If that person also has dimples there will be double crescent shapes at the mouth corners.

If I must do teeth, I would prefer not to make each individual tooth. I think it suffices to have a wedge of white or off-white for the upper teeth and ignore the lower teeth unless a really visible amount of the lower teeth are showing; for the lower teeth a narrow wedge of a very light gray will do. The rest of the mouth recedes back into darkness—a dark gray or charcoal will do for making this look proper.

Camille Vlasak has put a wonderful smile on her son, Connor, in her quilt *Waiting for Spring* on page 37. Connor has a very mischievous grin on his face and Camille opted to make individual teeth. She also included a highlight on his lips that make them look wet and glossy (works great for lips; however, you don't want noses to look wet and glossy).

Elvis and the Penguins, 1994, 53" x 53", Nancy S. Brown, Oakland, California (courtesy American Quilter's Society; photo by Charles R. Lynch). This tongue-in-cheek portrait of Elvis Presley was derived from several photos of him as well as were the penguins. This is the story Nancy tells with the quilt: "It is a little known fact that before Elvis became famous he toured the country with a highly talented group of penguins. Petty jealousies and squabbles over the nightly meal eventually led the band to break up. The penguins went home to Argentina and Elvis…well he became Elvis. Recent rumors have surfaced suggesting that Elvis is indeed alive and living in Argentina with his old friends. The penguins have no comment.

The Gospel According to the Choir, 1994, 68" x 98", Rebekka Seigel, Owenton, Kentucky (photo by Reba Rye). This quilt contains stylized depictions of faces and figures in the joyous act of singing.

Waiting for Spring, 1997, 30" x 31", Camille Vlasak, Collierville, Tennessee (photo by Thomas Anastasion). On a spring break trip to Ohio, the snow had melted and everything had turned to mud. In taking the photograph, Camille caught her son, Connor, sitting on the front steps looking out and just itching to get out in it. You can tell by the devilish look on his face he was in that mud very soon.

EARS

Ears are the least defining features of a face. How many people do you know that you could recognize by looking at their ears? It's important to have ears on the face if they are visible in the photograph, I don't sweat over the shapes that make up the ear as much as I do other parts of the face. You have to be careful because the shapes in ears are complicated and the contours can twist around in such a way that you come up with shapes that double back on themselves. The layering from light to dark can also be thrown off in the ears because sometimes dark shapes overlap light shapes. I tend to simplify a lot when I trace the ears.

Most of the time ears will be put together as separate sections. If there is a line down the side of the face that defines the cheek from the ear, it should be sewn together independently of the face. But if the flesh tones of the cheek blend seamlessly into the ear itself, it will have to be worked the same time as the face.

OTHER FEATURES

Cheeks, chins, jawlines, temples, foreheads, are, for the most part, smooth and less intricate to draw than the features are. Look for significant value changes to determine where to draw lines. Unless you intend to embroider or quilt the lines in, wrinkles need to be portrayed as narrow channels which will be reverse appliquéd.

Now that I have discussed various facial features, there's a challenge for you on the next two pages—a sort of quiz to see if you can identify individual eyes, noses, mouths, and ears from the shapes I've drawn. In four sets are photos of five different people in one row. In the next row, in a different sequence, are the features I have drawn from those photos. See if you can match the drawing to the photo it was traced from. The answers are at the bottom of the page.

Answers for eye page:
A—5, B—1, C—4, D—2, E—3.

Answers for nose page:
A—5, B—4, C—2, D—1, E—3.

Answers for mouth page:
A—3, B—1, C—5, D—4, E—2.

Answers for ear page:
A—4, B—1, C—3, D—5, E—4.

Eyes

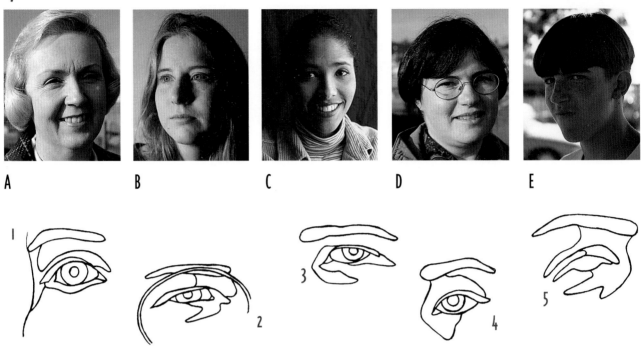

Noses

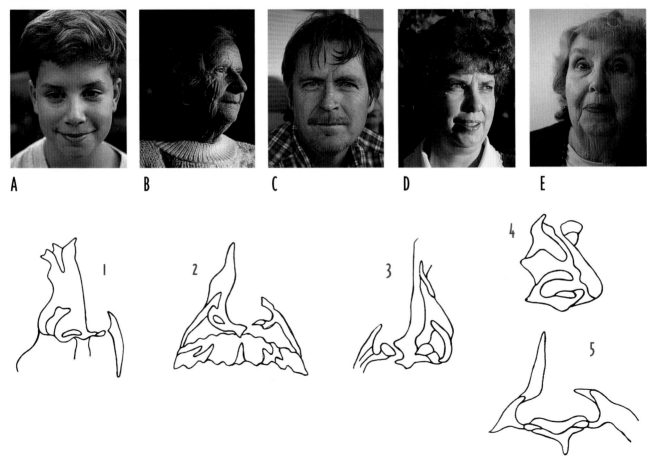

FOCUS ON FEATURES

Mouths

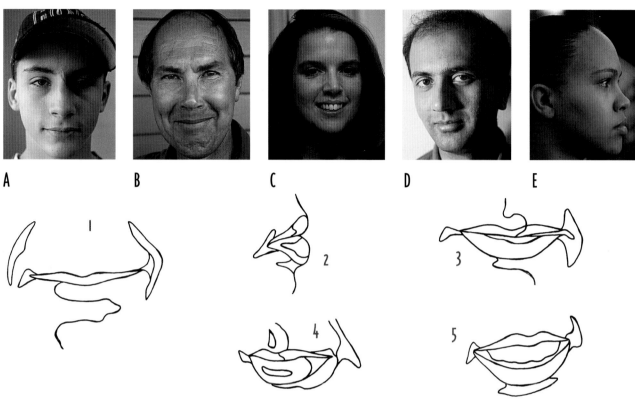

Ears

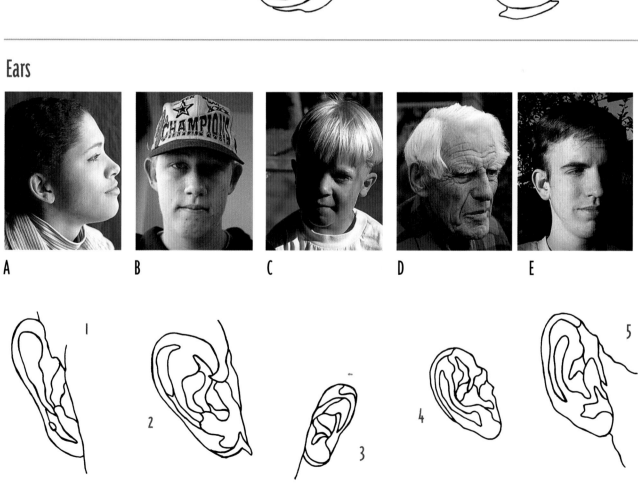

STITCHING AN EYE

Students are always intimidated by the size of the shapes within the drawn eye because they seem so tiny. But they are done with reverse appliqué which makes these shapes very do-able. Here is the step-by-step sequence for putting an eye together. (Eye number four from the quiz will be demonstrated.)

First of all, establish all flesh tones; the eye is recessed into the head so all shapes that make up the skin must be present so the eye can then be reverse appliquéd into the face. Using a lightbox, trace the pattern onto a flesh-tone fabric.

EYE 1

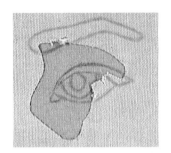

Reverse appliqué shadow around eyes, then return to lightbox and redraw any missing lines.

EYE 2

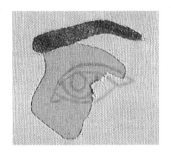

Reverse appliqué the eyebrow in it's place by pinning a swatch of the selected eyebrow fabric behind the work. (Some would rather appliqué the eyebrow on top and you can do this if it makes more sense to you. I would rather reverse it because I am guaranteed a more precise placement and the finished eyebrow is smooth rather than lumpy, as it would be if seam allowances were pushed under the eyebrow piece.) Cut down the center of the eyebrow shape which is drawn on the flesh tones, turn these edges under and stitch in place.

EYE 3

Eyelashes are next in the sequence for two reasons: 1) they protrude out in front of your eye and in real space are on top of the other components of the eye, and 2) the lash shape touches more of the outside edge of the total eye shape than any of the other pieces.

Pin a swatch of the fabric selected for the eyelash behind the eye shape. Cut through the middle of the eye shape and into the corners. Clip the upper curve of the eye shape so the edge will turn under smoothly.

EYE 4

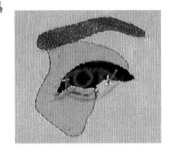

Stitch only where the eyelash shape touches the flesh tones. Baste the lower seam allowance to the eyelash fabric to keep the eye shape from stretching apart while the redrawing and trimming is done. Place the piece back on the lightbox on top of the pattern and redraw the bottom line of the eyelash and any of the rest of the eye that is missing on the eyelash fabric. Trim the excess eyelash fabric from behind the piece.

EYE 5

The white of the eye comes next because, of all the pieces left (white, iris, pupil), it has the most of its shape touching the edges of the flesh tones and the eyelash fabric. Pin a swatch of eye white fabric behind the face. Remove the basting from the previous step and trim the edges to a seam allowance, if necessary. Clip the curve of the lower lid. Stitch everywhere that the eye white touches the lower lid and the eyelash, making sure to leave openings for the iris and the tiny pink tear duct at the corner. Place the piece back on the lightbox on top of the pattern and redraw any missing lines on the eye white. Trim away the excess eye-white fabric from behind the piece.

EYE 6

The iris is done next by pinning a swatch of the iris fabric behind the piece. Cut carefully into the iris shape of the eye-white fabric, clipping about every ⅛ inch to get a nice, round curve to the iris. Turn these clips under carefully to reveal the iris fabric. Stitch everywhere the iris shape touches the eyelash, eye white, and flesh tones. In this example the iris does not touch the flesh tone because the eye is looking up slightly, and the pupil is touching the eyelash. An opening needs to be left here so that the pupil may be reverse appliquéd in. Place the piece back on the lightbox on top of the pattern and redraw the pupil on the iris fabric. Trim the excess iris fabric away from behind the piece.

EYE 7

Pin a small piece of black fabric behind the piece to make the pupil. Make tiny clips in the iris fabric revealing the black fabric underneath. Stitch around this tiny circular shape. Trim away the excess pupil fabric from behind the piece. You may be tempted to use a permanent marker and ink in the pupil. This is acceptable. However, I think the appliquéd pupil looks much more dimensional.

EYE 8

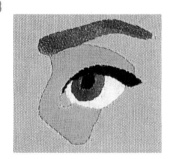

There is still the tear duct to do. But, it can only be done if you have left an opening for it. Pin a swatch of pink fabric behind the piece. You shouldn't have to do any clipping if you have already cut into the corner of the eye. Turn under any raw or unsewn edges, revealing the pink fabric, and sew these edges down. Trim away any excess pink fabric.

EYE 9

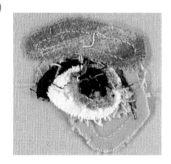

The back side looks strange but has no extra fabric.

If you have carefully observed the way a sculptor has portrayed an eye in a statue, it is layered much the same way as this reverse appliqué is done. Each successive layer is carved out of the clay, stone, or other material, in the order I have listed above. By carving downward this way, a sculptor can come up with a realistic simulation of an eye.

STITCHING A MOUTH

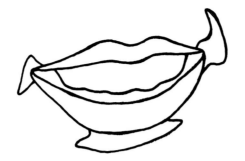

The mouth is put together very similarly to an eye in that all the parts are reverse appliquéd after the flesh tones are established. You may want to appliqué the lips on top of the flesh tones, especially if you are going for a "pouty" look, but then you have to worry about being very careful in your placement. Pieces that are added on top tend to move out of place more than if they are reverse appliquéd. Everything behind the lips should be reverse appliquéd. This step-by-step will demonstrate mouth number five from the quiz.

MOUTH 1

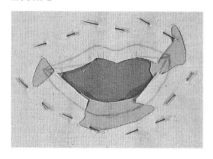

Since the smile lines at the corner of the mouth are flesh tones, they need to be reverse appliquéd in first as does the shadow under the bottom lip. Pin a piece of the appropriate flesh tone behind the piece and stitch everywhere these shapes touch the other flesh tones. Do not stitch anywhere these shapes touch the shapes of the mouth. Baste to hold together any large openings and trim the excess fabric away from behind the piece. Redraw any missing mouth lines onto the fabric you have just added.

MOUTH 2

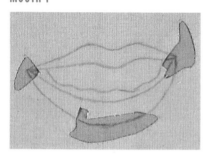

I will be making the upper lip a darker color than the lower lip. Pin a swatch of the darker lip fabric, big enough to cover the whole mouth, behind the piece. Cut through the middle of the mouth, into the corners, and trim the upper lip line to a seam allowance.

MOUTH 3

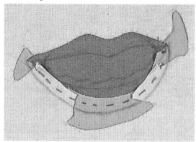

Turn the seam under and stitch from corner to corner along the top line of the upper lip. Cut a seam allowance above the bottom line of the lower lip and baste this edge in place. Place the piece on the lightbox on top of the pattern and redraw the missing lines of the mouth. Trim the excess upper lip fabric from behind the piece.

MOUTH 4

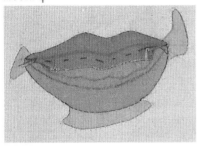

The lower lip will be done next. Pin a swatch of the lower lip fabric behind the piece. Remove the basting and trim the upper lip fabric the width of a seam allowance below the bottom line of the upper lip. Turn under the flesh-tone fabric seam allowance for the bottom line of the lower lip and stitch it in place from corner to corner. Baste down the seam allowance from the upper lip to the lower lip fabric. Place the piece on the lightbox on top of the pattern and redraw any missing lines for the mouth. Trim the excess lower lip fabric from behind the piece.

MOUTH 5

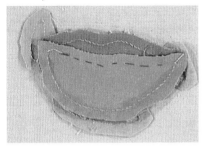

The back side looks like this at this stage.

MOUTH 6

The teeth are next. Pin a swatch of white fabric behind the piece. Remove the basting and trim the lower lip fabric to a seam allowance above the top line of the lower lip. Turn this seam allowance under if it is in the way. Turn under the seam allowance of the upper lip and stitch it only where the teeth shape touches the upper lip shape. Baste the lower lip to the white fabric with the seam allowance turned under. Place the piece on the lightbox on top of the pattern and redraw the shape of the teeth on the white fabric. Trim away the excess white fabric from behind the piece.

MOUTH 7

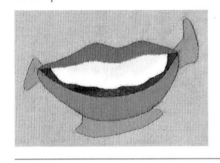

The last step is to stitch in the dark gray fabric to make the hollow of the mouth. Pin a piece of dark gray fabric behind the piece. Remove the basting and trim the white fabric to a seam allowance around the teeth shape. Turning under the seam allowances, stitch down all remaining free edges, changing thread to match the fabric you are stitching down as you work around the piece. Trim any excess dark gray fabric from behind the piece. The mouth is now complete.

MOUTH 8

This is the way the back side of the work should look.

Mouths can be drawn and stitched in a more complicated manner than the one I have just demonstrated. You just have to work out a layering sequence for each additional fabric color so that each element of the mouth is in its logical place.

Hand in Hand

"Anyone who has tried to draw the human figure has quickly learned that the hand is among the most complex of the body forms."
— Burne Hogarth

PORTRAYING HANDS

When people ask me why I make the type of quilts I do, I usually tell them it's because I believe that, when using the fabric medium, a face is the greatest challenge one can undertake. It's a lie. The ultimate challenge is faithfully portraying a hand. It is a challenge for painters and sculptors. It is even more difficult to do in fabric and thread.

It's not that you can't make a hand with appliqué—all you need to do is trace around the shape of your hand, transfer that shape onto fabric, stitch it in place, and everyone will recognize it as a representation of a human hand. It's portraying a hand that is shaded and dimensional and made out of tiny sections of various colors of fabric that makes for a demanding achievement.

The hand is a complicated mechanism. It has twenty-seven bones that give it structure. These bones are covered with a myriad of muscles, sinews, veins, and tendons that provide further shape and form to the hand. The hand spreads into five appendages, each with several joints. As the muscles move the various parts of the hand around, each section interplays differently with the light. Sit next to a window or a lamp and move your hand around under the light and notice where the light and shadow falls. The high or "out" parts of your hand receive the most light—knuckles, the ball of the thumb, finger pads, etc. The lines and creases or "in" parts on the palm create shadows and shadows define the separations between your fingers. Watch the shapes in your hand change as it moves; look for form shadows and cast shadows. Your hand is very intricate, is it not?

I must confess that, if left with an option, I would rather not do hands in appliqué. In giving that statement, I was surprised to look back over the quilts I have and see how many hands I had actually made. Given the fact that the hands I portrayed were small and not life-size, I am content, if not satisfied, with the way they turned out.

Of course, the smaller the hand is to be drawn, the less shape and dimension it can have for there is a limit on how small a piece can be appliquéd. (There is also a limit on the amount of patience one has for doing such a task.) For many smaller figures, an estimation of the hand or just an outline will do, but if the hand itself has any size to it at all, there needs to be some definition of light and shadow. My aim in tracing a hand is to make a resonable likeness, but still be able to stitch it in layers, using one piece of fabric for all the shapes of one color in each section.

I must admit that every time I have to draw hands, I groan inwardly and grit my teeth. Next to noses, this is where I use my eraser the most. The trick is to create a hand that has the proper number of digits in relation to its angle.

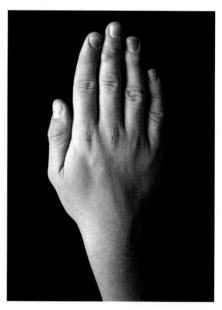

Closed fingers

Achieving shadows and finger separation can depend on the position of the fingers. In the photograph of the hand the fingers and thumb are closed—pulled up next to each other so the hand has to be dealt with as a whole even though fingers have

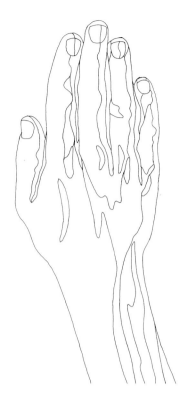

In the photograph the fingers are spread. This makes for an easier portrayal. The fingers can be dealt with as serarate entities instead of looking at them lying right next to each other. Again, this photograph was projected to life-size and the drawing was traced from it.

The drawing is still very complicated, but would actually be easier to work in appliqué than the first one. If I were to opt to do it in a smaller size, I would not have to simplify it as much; I could still keep most of the shapes.

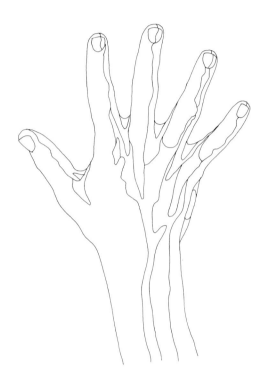

separations between them. The shadows between these appendages become very narrow.

The drawing I have done from this photograph was done with the photograph projected to life-size. At this size the shapes are do-able but very testing. If I were to do this hand in any smaller size, I would have to eliminate many of the shapes.

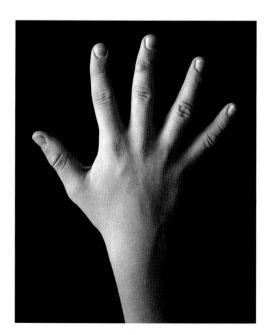

Open fingers

FORESHORTENING

Foreshortening in hands creates many drawing problems. The first relatively realistic rendering I did of hands was in my quilt *She Comes In Colors*. I simplified these hands as much as I could, and as I said, I am content with them for I was able to layer these hands without breaking them into smaller sections, and they have as small pieces as I really want to work with. It is not a great portrayal of hands but it will do.

The drawing shows these hands at 50% of the actual size I worked them. Notice the foreshortening, which is my attempt at spatial recession. The fingers of the right hand are bent at the knuckles and the first joint of each finger is only visible as one shadow. The thumb is curled in and overshadowed. The middle finger is curled inward more than the others and that is why it is so much longer. The middle finger of the left hand is also curled in more than the others so it becomes a dark shadow. The forearm is coming at you with a downward slant and is very foreshortened.

The photograph of the hand was taken so the foreshortening would be very apparent. The hand was laid flat on the table and the camera angle was only slightly above it.

If you trace the outline of this hand, it takes on a fairly bizarre configuration; the thumb looks as long as the fingers.

It is the shadows and shapes that bring it to life and make it look like a real hand instead of a misshapen blob.

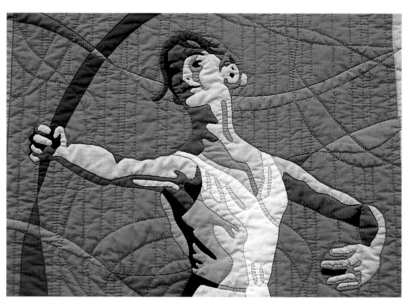

Detail of hands in *She Comes In Colors* 1988, 72" x 48", Charlotte Warr Andersen, Salt Lake City, Utah (photo by Borge Andersen).

50% of actual size.

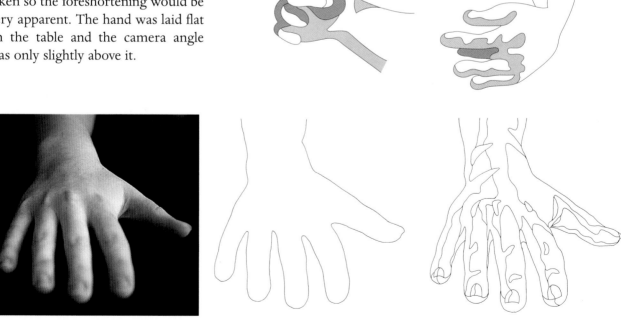

Foreshortened hand

AGEING

Hands change drastically as we age. Baby hands are tiny and pink and we marvel over how small and delicate they are. The fingers are short, the muscles can be plump and rounded, the knuckles are not all that apparent. Because they are so small in the first place, it is difficult to portray them with shading even at life-size.

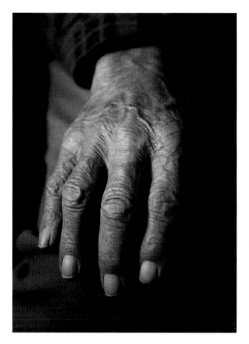 

Fingers lengthen, muscles become less fleshy, and the hand develops more capacities as we grow older. Differences are apparent at almost every age level and the older they get the more character they take on.

As we become aged our hands begin to lose some of their substance. The skin becomes somewhat translucent, muscles lose their tone, and veins protrude. These conditions create many more complications in the portrayal of this type of hand. Some of those

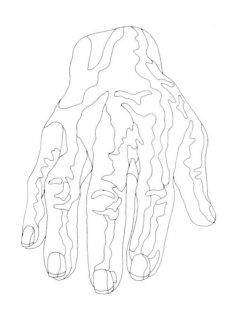 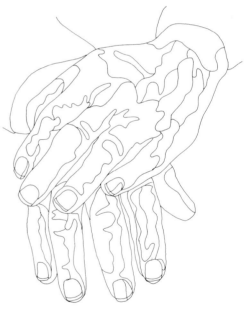

complications include age spots, blue-colored veins, wrinkles and lots of them. Many of these things can be changed or ignored, but some of them need to be portrayed to be in keeping with the age of the subject.

The photographs above are of my 83-year-old father-in-law's hands. A ship builder and a gardener by trade, his hands have years of experience carved into them. I have done a slightly larger than life-size projection of this photograph and traced from it. I have ignored many of the wrinkles and color changes.

The resulting drawing is very complicated with lines wavering everywhere, twisting in and out, and so many inside and outside points to appliqué!

I have another picture that shows one hand over the other. Here I projected the photograph to life-size and simplified a bit more than I did for the single hand. The drawing is still very complicated, and with two hands instead of one there is almost twice as much work to do. As beautiful as these hands are to me, duplicating this photograph in fabric would be a crowning acheivement and maybe one day I will be up for it.

OCCUPIED HANDS

Hands have the potential for being every bit as expressive as a face, and they are much more dramatic when they are doing something. Posing, pointing, gesticulating, working, holding, and grasping are some activities that can occupy hands. Here are three examples of hands that are in action.

The first is a photograph of my daughter, Aubry, (or her hand, I should say) working on one of her drawings. Simple window light was my light source and the camera is on the opposite side, which gives backlighting and most of the hand is dark. I projected the photograph at about three quarters life-size.

The drawing is relatively simple, though there are some fairly small shapes. The shadows need to curve around the knuckles where they are bending to grasp the pencil, otherwise the fingers would look lopped off. The pencil is a good prop and its yellow color makes for an interesting color change.

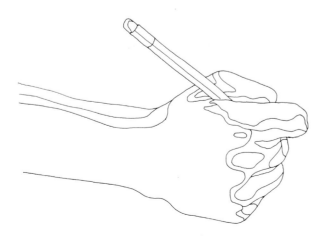

The next two photographs show my son Davyn's hand holding a shiny, red apple. In the first of these two examples, foreshortening is apparent in the back of his hand. His fingers cover much of the apple, rendering the red shape harder to define as being an apple. Notice the brightest light is hitting his fingertips. In the second picture, Davyn is cradling the apple in his hand and this time you can definitely tell it is an apple. I pulled his forefinger out from the apple and had him point it just before I took the photograph to make the composition much more interesting. Unfortunately, the photograph is slightly out of focus but it's still useable. (As a matter of fact, it is hard to have the whole of the subject matter in focus when you are doing close-ups like this—notice the apple stem is in focus.) I have done slightly larger than life-size drawings of both of these pictures.

Of the two, I'm much more inclined to actually stitch the second one. The shapes are much more intriguing and descriptive.

These hand drawings may look very intimidating to you. But they are rather extreme examples. An appealing hand can be done yet still be rather simple. One hand that I have done in fabric that I'm actually willing to brag about is the hand of the girl in my quilt *Naiad*.

The pattern is quite simple with three flesh tones used. Even with this minimum number of shades the hand has dimension and it looks like her fingers curl around the cup she is holding. The transparency of the cup itself was accomplished with several layers of white silk organza and gold lamé.

I hope that with this discussion I have not dissuaded you from attempting to portray hands. I have shown examples of both the simple and complicated variety. If the focus of your quilt is not the hands, you do not need to go to all that much work. But if you do include hands in your piece they need to be identifiable and relate well with the other areas of flesh tones in the amount of shadow and dimension they have. In other words, if the face in your quilt has three or four flesh tones in it, don't make the hands just one flesh tone—they will look neglected and skipped-over.

Naiad, 1994, 60" x 60", Charlotte Warr Andersen, Salt Lake City, Utah (photo by Thomas Anastasion).

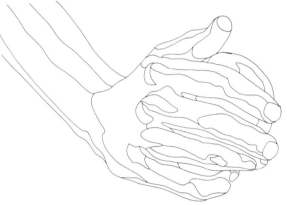

Detail of hand in *Naiad*.

Shown at 40% of actual size drawing.

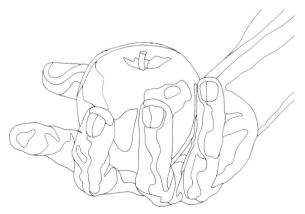

David Ben-Gurion, 1994, 30" x 34", Avril Bright, Ottawa, Ontario, Canada (photo by Myron Miller). Ben-Gurion, who dedicated his life to establishing a Jewish homeland in Palestine, was the first prime minister of Israel and is regarded as the father of his country. This portrait, worked from a famous copyrighted photograph by Shabtai Tal and used with his permission, is beautifully done and is highlighted by thoughtful, expressive hands.

Ki Tetzeh, 1994, 33" x 48", D. J. Berger, Santa Rosa, California (photo by Thomas Anastasion). The title of the quilt is the Hebrew name of the portion of the Bible D.J.'s son, Adam, chanted for his Bar Mitzvah. He holds a kiddush cup (wine goblet) to bless wine, and the fringes are ritually tied in a special way to remember the commandments. Background quilting is part of the Hebrew text of Ki Tetzeh.

Mountain Dollmaker, 1989, 39" x 34", Rebekka Seigel, Owenton, Kentucky (photo by Jay Bachemin). Based on a photograph taken by Doris Ullman in the 30's, this portrait of a woman carving a doll is placed in front of the traditional Flying Geese pattern. It is a simple depiction of aged hands at work.

Indiana Memories, 1994, 60" x 70", Marlene Brown Woodfield, La Porte, Indiana (photo by Marlene Brown Woodfield). This is a scenic portrait of Marin and Leah, Marlene's daughters, at the beach. Marlene prefers using subtle print fabrics for her flesh tones and feels that it is an easy way to blend one color with another.

Animals, Friendly and Wild

"It is more intelligent to accept what the eye finds and then try to deduce the reason. It is not a very good approach to tell nature what it ought to look like."
—Ted Seth Jacobs, *Light for the Artist*

Presenting our furry, feathered, and scaled friends presents new challenges for us quilters. Simple shapes and silhouettes can intimate at bears, horses, dogs, birds, etc., but this book is about achieving shading and dimension and attempting to re-create reality. You can come up with an outline of a moose, make it out of brown fabric and appliqué it in place, and people will recognize that it looks like a moose. But if you want the viewer to say, "Wow! That looks just like a moose!" you are going to have to do a lot more work.

Animals come in an endless array of colors, textures, and sizes. Some are untamed creatures that we view mostly from a distance or in pens or cages, while some are our housemates and we love them like family. Similar to creating a portrait of a human, an animal portrait is also a labor of love.

TEXTURE

One of the first things you may want to consider is the texture of your chosen animal. Let's not look with our eyes but with our fingertips for a moment. For example: frogs, salamanders, worms, and the like have smooth slippery skin; some might consider them slimy creatures. Fish are slippery but they have scales that you can feel the edge of when rubbing "against their grain." Snakes and lizards also have scales, but are dry feeling if the creature doesn't live in the water. Birds have feathers (which are scales that have evolved into something more specialized) and depending on which part of the bird you are touching, can feel fluffy, soft, insubstantial, or crisp and brittle. Mammals have hair but the quality and texture of that hair varies greatly. Horses have comparatively short hair (except for their mane and tails), which thickens out to become longer when the weather is cold; when the hair is short it adds very little to the actual shape of the body. There are shaggy mammals like llamas and musk oxen where the hair makes up a substantial part of their shape. Whales

and dolphins are mammals but we don't think of them as having hair at all.

Such diversity in the animal kingdom makes for an interesting mental game to play: What does an animal feel like and how would one portray it in fabric? (Even if you haven't felt a scaly anteater, and I haven't, it's intriguing to imagine the sensation of feeling such a beast.) This texture game aids me in deciding what lines I will draw and in choosing what fabrics I will use for an animal portrait.

COLOR

Now let's discuss color. There is such variety in the world of living things that you only have to pick a color and there is an animal that will be that color. While mammals tend to stick to the more earthy tones, because one of the purposes of hair is for camouflage with natural surroundings, you will not lack if you long to work in saturated colors. If you feel like working in electric blue and gold, there is a macaw that color. Frogs and toads come in a rainbow of hues. There are fish, insects, and worms in neon, glow-in-the-dark colors. Quilters are fortunate that the fabric manufacturers have provided us with such an array of fabrics that we may depict anything we choose in the way of color.

If the animal you choose to depict is small and not much detail is included, one or two fabric colors may do. But if you are portraying your subject of choice in large size or a close-up view, and want to make it look shaded and dimensional, you need to have several values of each of the colors you choose to work with. And most animals are multicolored beings.

At the Waterhole, 1995, 60" x 52", Nancy S. Brown, Oakland, California (photo by Nancy Brown). This is one of Nancy's multi-animal quilts. When the animals are smaller, not as much detail can be incorporated in the figures. The lions are in front sleeping behind the grass, otherwise the other animals wouldn't be there.

ing but texture. Its skin is cracked and wrinkled and scored, and there are fine lines everywhere on an elephant's body. In this case, it is appropriate to use fabrics that imitate that wrinkled and fissured look.

Most animals, however, have more than one color on their bodies and those colors intertwine and variegate. The general texture may stay the same over the surface of an animal's body but there are some where it changes; like short smooth hair on some parts of the body and long, shaggy hair on other parts. Nancy Brown's *Orangutan* quilt is a case in point; an orangutan has parts of its body that have little or no hair and the other parts, like its arms, have hair that is long and stringy.

It is truly a challenge to portray that interchange of colors and textures and then to have the animal forms shaded and dimensional besides. The fabric shopping/search may be just as much a challenge as the actual creation of the quilt.

In Tandem

Put color and texture together and the formula changes. The two need to work together to make a reasonable depiction. We humans, being smoothed skinned, are basically one color except for hair, eyes, clothing, and other adornments, of course. That is why I almost always opt to make my flesh tones out of solids. Solids give me the uniform look that I want. Animals, on the other hand, seem the perfect choice for using textures. I am not talking about using fabric with actual textures like velvet, fake-fur, or burlap (though if you think you can make those fabrics work, go for it!). What I am referring to is using printed textures and two-dimensional prints that simulate the characteristics of the creatures we are trying to portray.

There are animals that could be considered to be all of one color. An elephant is what most of us would consider to be all gray, for instance, and seen from a far distance, very little in the way of texture is apparent. So, if you are including an elephant in a landscape quilt, and it is in the distance, making it out of solid grays would be appropriate. But seen up close, an elephant is noth-

Orangutan, 1996, 52" x 52", Nancy S. Brown, Oakland, California (photo by Nancy Brown). Nancy says, "I made this quilt because I wanted to do a close-up of one animal to show the detail of the face and fur and hands, etc. ...It has always been one of my favorite animals." She took her own photos at several zoos to base this quilt on and the background came from her imagination.

PETS

You may be a cat lover, a bird enthusiast, a dog fanatic or some other type of animal owner; but having a non-human household member may be the perfect opportunity for making a quilt. Here are three examples of quilters who have made pet portraits. Susan Brown began her quilt in one of my Appliqué for Realism workshops. Mr. Festus is a beautiful calico cat and this close-up view of him is wonderfully reproduced in delicately textured fabrics. In *Cockatiels* by Janet Liang the birds are depicted in a variety of colors that are mostly solid fabrics but with a hint of texture here and there. Carol Goddu's Springer Spaniel looks quite noble and is exquisitely stitched in a variety of textured print fabrics.

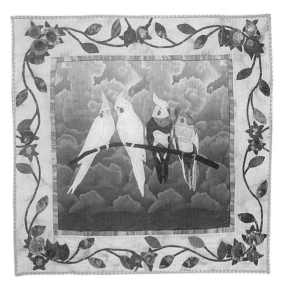

Cockatiels, 1997, 37" x 37", Janet Liang, Banchiau, Taipei, Taiwan (photo by Beckon Studio Co., Ltd.). Janet writes, "The cockatiels are my favorite pets. They accompany and share all my emotions in this journey of life. When there was a chance in my devoted quilt class to create my own pictorial design, the idea of making my feathered friends jumped out of my mind instantly.

Mr. Festus, 1996, 22" x 35", Susan E. Brown, Durham, North Carolina (photo by Seth Tyson-Lewis). Susan states the she doesn't usually do hand appliqué. This was a *"labor of love"* inspired by her photograph of her cat.

Arrangement in Brown and White, 1996, 40" x 50", Carol Goddu, Mississauga, Ontario, Canada (photo by Alan McKenzie). Carol has been doing pictorial appliqué for fifteen years and this is her first portrait of a member of the family. Inspirational images came from photos of her Springer Spaniel, calendars, pet guides and greeting cards.

I happen to be an admirer of dogs and have two canine family members, so I am using them as examples of drawing animal patterns. Both of them are mixed-breed dogs; we acquired Betsy through an acquaintance and I found Scruffy at the county animal shelter. My family loves them both dearly. Scruffy thinks he's quite human and longs for his own chair at the dinner table while Betsy is high-strung but well-mannered and is an excellent watch dog.

Scruffy

Scruffy is basically a white dog (though he is a dirt magnet and that is how he got his name). He also has touches of cream or beige here and there; like his ears, tail, and a skunk-like stripe of it down his back, but this color is light enough that it can be somewhat ignored. Since he is basically one color, he is relatively easy to portray with different values of white ranging into beiges and almost brown.

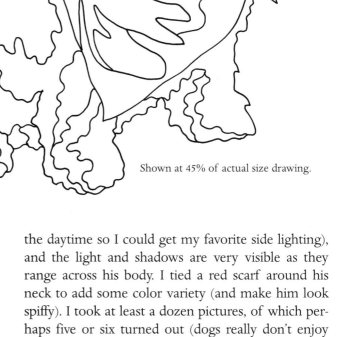

Shown at 45% of actual size drawing.

Scruffy had just been groomed (my friend, Joan Rollins, can make him look absolutely adorable) and I took the opportunity to take pictures of him. I covered a piece of furniture with black fabric, draped black fabric behind him (next to a window during the daytime so I could get my favorite side lighting), and the light and shadows are very visible as they range across his body. I tied a red scarf around his neck to add some color variety (and make him look spiffy). I took at least a dozen pictures, of which perhaps five or six turned out (dogs really don't enjoy having their pictures taken).

I noticed that Scruffy actually has two different textures, or types of hair on his body. He has the short curly hair (because it has been cut) which has been combed, brushed, and fussed with until it's really poofy, and he has the longer, stringier hair on his ears, snout, and tail. I have traced different types of shapes for these different textures of hair. Along his legs, back, and body, the lines I've drawn are bumpy and wiggly to denote that poofy hair. For the ears, snout, and tail, the lines are longer and sometimes wavy with points here and there, and the lengthier parts of the shapes I've drawn follow the direction of the hair. I projected this photograph at about two-thirds Scruffy's actual size when doing the drawing. The drawing is a bit complicated at this size but if I enlarged it to full size it would be more workable.

Betsy

Betsy is a different sort of dog, so in portraying her more problems arise. For one thing, she has two distinct colors of white and reddish-brown. This means I will need to have several values of white for her white areas and several values of red-brown for her reddish-brown areas. Many more shapes to draw in other words. She also has differently textured hair than Scruffy does. I have never had her professionally groomed because she doesn't really require it like

Scruffy does. She has long, fine hair on most of her body (and sheds horribly) that falls victim to static electricity a lot, so she has these stray ends poking out everywhere. The only way I can portray these spiky hairs if I don't want to embroider or thread -paint is by appliquéing dagger points (thin, long, tapering points). Dagger points are the things I least enjoy appliquéing.

I had a student who brought a picture to class of her Yorkshire Terrier and wanted to create a quilt of this dog. A Yorky has spiky little points everywhere on its body. I helped her draw a pattern for her dog and after we were finished the pattern had what I would guess to be 1,000 dagger points on it. She spent most of an afternoon stitching on it and got

maybe 12 to 15 points done. The next morning she had decided to change projects and came to class with a picture of a tree frog; only a few dagger points on this one. I'm not saying you can't do dagger points; just realize that they are a lot more work, and be patient if you're going to attempt such a portrait.

Back to Betsy, I took pictures of her at the same time I took photographs of Scruffy. Betsy likes to have her picture taken even less than Scruffy does and only a few turned out of her. (I'm lucky I got her to sit still at all.)

I projected the slide of Betsy to her full size. Trying to simplify as much as I could and still get a shaded and dimensional figure, the shapes and the whole drawing, for that matter, are still quite complicated. And there are lots of dagger points because Betsy would not look like Betsy otherwise. I'm not sure I would want to do Betsy in hand appliqué. For her, I may be tempted to lay down all the shapes in the appropriate color of fabric, fuse them in place with WonderUnder® and then thread-paint over the top of it.

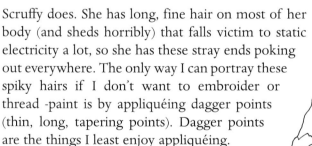

Shown at 30% of actual size drawing.

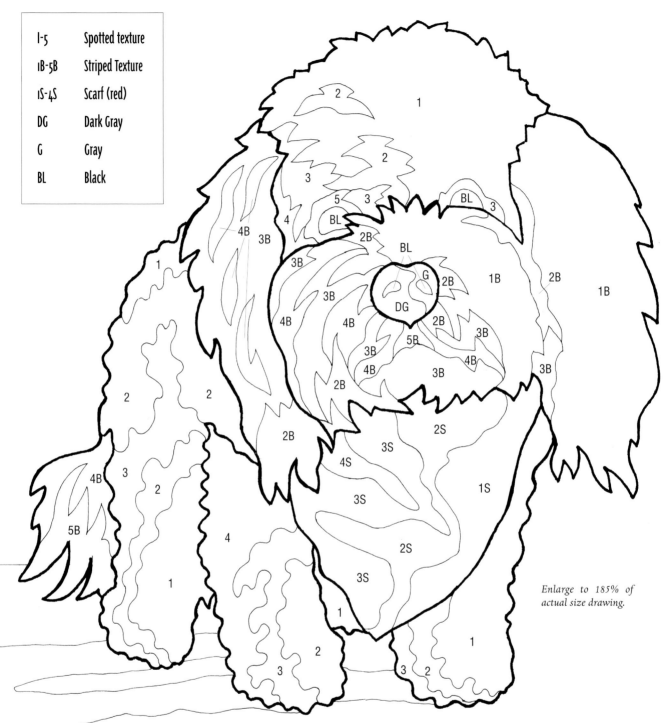

1-5	Spotted texture
1B-5B	Striped Texture
1S-4S	Scarf (red)
DG	Dark Gray
G	Gray
BL	Black

Enlarge to 185% of actual size drawing.

STITCHING SCRUFFY

To give you an example of how I would put together a pet portrait, I have worked up an appliqué of Scruffy. This pattern is not the same one as shown on page 56. At the same time I took the slides of Scruffy I took some prints. I liked the print photograph I took of my dog better that any of the slides and if I'm actually going to stitch something I had better

like it. So that is why this pattern is different; it is truly simpler than the other pattern.

This portrait of Scruffy is relatively easy to do at life-size. If you would like to do it as well, enlarge it at 185%. Since Scruffy has two different textures to his fur, I picked out two sets of prints that had five values going from white to light brown. The first set of prints were of a spotty or dotted texture to simulate the short, poofy hair. The second set of prints had a lined texture to them — nothing symmetric —

Scruffy in sections

Scruffy assembled

with the lightest fabric, working down through each shade and stitching only where that fabric connects to the previous shade—leaving generous seam allowances around the outside edges, until all the shapes in each section have been completed.

The photograph shows all the sections of Scruffy complete; edges have been trimmed to a ¼" seam allowance where they are to be sewn on top of other sections or down to the background, generous seam allowances are left where sections overlap, and the eyes have been reverse appliquéd into his face.

These sections are now sewn together and Scruffy has his complete form with seam allowances all the way around.

Now I prepare a background to put him on. I just have two colors to create a dividing line for what he is standing on, and the drape behind him and reverse appliqué a shadow into it. Then I stitch him to the background and trim away the excess background fabric from behind the dog. My portrait of Scruffy is complete.

One other note about his eyes: in the photograph I could distinctly see a bright highlight in his left eye and thought I needed it. Using white and/or gray thread, I tried to satin stitch this highlight into his eye three different ways. It never looked good. It always made Scruffy look dumber than he actually is and I decided the portrait looked better without the highlight.

Completed Scruffy

but lines nonetheless to give the look of hairs crisscrossing over each other. The lightest value in each set were white-on-white fabrics.

The pattern is broken down into workable sections, the bold lines indicating the different sections: the top of his head, his left ear together with his snout, his nose, his right ear, the scarf, his left front leg, his left back leg (which is only one piece of number one white fabric), his right front leg, his left back leg and rear end, and his tail. Each of these sections is worked with the reverse layering process starting

SPOTTED AND STRIPED ANIMALS

Again, getting into more complications, you have to consider depicting animals that have spots or stripes as some of their main features. You could just use fabric (there are plenty of animal print fabrics available on the market). But there are problems with using them. One is that they won't necessarily be in the scale or size you desire. The other problem is that in using a preprinted fabric, the fabric will dictate where those spots and stripes lay.

If you want a more realistic depiction, you will have to consider creating your own spots and stripes. Nancy S. Brown has done just that in her close-up portrayals of a jaguar and giraffes.

In *Jaguar*, we see that Nancy has done a magnificent job portraying this sleek cat. Its pelt has been shaded and variegated using multiple prints with subtle textures. But most amazing, its spots are all in the right places and they vary in shape according to size, location, and perspective. Most of the black parts have been reverse appliquéd after the other shapes have been established.

Giraffes have much larger spots. Here each spot has been created out of several textured fabrics (some which are spotted themselves) and these spots and the light body behind them are shaded precisely around the contours of each neck. These giraffes are painstakingly and lovingly done but the work is most definitely worth it.

Jaguar, 1996, 46" x 50", Nancy S. Brown, Oakland, California (photo by Thomas Anastasion). Nancy has made several quilts with myriad animals in them. Often she makes quilts of single animals so the she can show a lot of the detail she has to eliminate in her multi-animal quilts. This is a very intricate study of this large cat.

Giraffes, 1997, 70" x 50", Nancy S. Brown, Oakland, California (photo by Thomas Anastasion). Another of Nancy's awesome animal artworks. About this quilt she writes, "When I was a child I visited the Portland Zoo. They had a giraffe exhibit where you could walk up a hill and look at the giraffes eye to eye. I loved seeing the giraffes so close and that visit so many years ago was the inspiration for this quilt."

Duet #2, 1997, 72" x 90", Caryl Bryer Fallert, Oswego, Illinois (photo by Caryl Bryer Fallert). Caryl began making this quilt after almost losing her husband, Bob, to a ruptured blood vessel in his brain. She writes, "Birds of all kinds have become personal symbols for the many events and relationships in my life. This is one of several quilts about birds that mate for life." Hand-dyed, hand-painted, machine pieced, appliquéd and quilted, the eagles entertwine beautifully on the swirling colors of the background.

Color Makes the Difference

"We each have our own sensitivity to beauty, color and creative imagery. The designs that appeal to us, the way we strive to put colors together, the textures we choose - there are no rights or wrongs."
—Joen Wolfrom, *The Magical Effects of Color*

VALUE

In general terms the word "value" means the worth of a thing. The word has more specific meanings for mathematics, music, phonetics, and art. For the artist or quiltmaker, it pertains to the relative lightness or darkness of a color. It seems to me that for success in this "drawing turned into appliqué" process, which I have been discussing for the last several chapters, it is the weightier of all the terms that relate to color in art.

As I gaze out my window today, thinking about how to express this concept of value, I am looking upon a white world. Salt Lake City has had a major snowstorm in the last two days. Those two days were rather miserable indoors, for the house was dark from lack of window light, but it was better than being outside. Outside the snow was blowing everywhere; it was cold and you wanted to keep your eyes closed against the wind and moisture that was blowing in your face. Driving in the car, while worrisome because of safety concerns, one had the sensation of being boxed or closed in. The weather limited visibility to a few feet in front and everything looked flat, gray, and depressing; visually, my surroundings lacked value.

Overnight, it has changed and the world is beautiful again. The sun is shining, the snow sparkling, the driveways and roads have been cleared. What I see out the window is mostly white since snow covers everything, so the scene I am observing is high in value. But since the sun is out and shining brightly, shadows are falling everywhere. Middle value shadows define where walkways have been carved out of seven inches of snow. Dark, blue-gray shadows of trees fall across flat expanses of snowfall. Building shadows and the underside of cars are almost black.

Yesterday, looking out the window, the cherry trees in my yard would have been discernable only by the outline of their shape (if I could see them through the falling snow at all); they would have looked flat and all one color or value. Today they look shaded and dimensional. They are mostly all one color since they are leafless this time of year, but as the sunlight is cast about them you can see several values of the purply-gray that they are. Each trunk and branch is very light gray on the side that is facing the sun and middle to dark gray on the side that is in shadow with various values in between. The world is so much more pleasurable to view with light falling on it. Observation of the values that the light creates will bring a scene or portrait to life.

So, while you are drawing or tracing from a photograph you need to look for ways to separate these values with a line and to keep in mind what those values are. Once the lines are in place, you need to

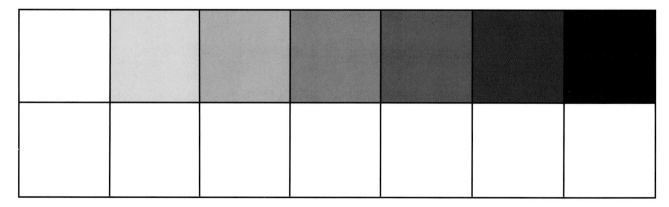

Value Boxes

assign a color and value to each shape. One of the things I usually do after completing the drawing is to shade in the areas or shapes according to value with my pencil. The following is an exercise to give you an idea of how this works. Perhaps you are drawing a subject that has seven different shades of one color. Take a series of seven adjoining boxes; the first box is white or your highest value, the last or seventh box is the darkest, or lowest value. Start with the second box and use a soft lead pencil; color in that box, softly creating a very light gray, then color the next box slightly darker, and the next darker, until in the seventh box you are pressing with your pencil as hard as the paper will allow. This last box could possibly turn out black.

This is essentially what I do with my pattern drawings. I put a number designating value, one being the lightest and so on, in each shape and then shade it in with my pencil accordingly. You can do this with colored pencils or paint in the appropriate color if you want to, but I find a pencil adequate for indicating values. Do not color too darkly on the actual pattern you are using for transferring the shapes to fabric, or you will not be able to see the lines when you trace from the lightbox.

Developing this sense of value is very important. In my workshop, I request that students bring four to six shades of gray ranging from light to dark. I have them bring grays because they are the easiest fabrics to make look right. Many students bring three light grays and two dark, or five middle-value grays plus black or other combinations that do not have this shade-by-shade value exchange. It is very difficult to have something turn out right if too many of the values are missing.

Once the value designations have been made, it is time to decide on the actual color.

Color—Right, Righter, Rightest?

So, how does one go about making the right color choice? That I cannot answer, because color preference is a totally personal choice. You can take classes or read about color theory, but all instructions about the use of color are theoretical and unprovable. Learning all about color is a worthy pursuit, but sometimes it is OK to ignore what has been learned. For every rule put forth about the right and wrong way to use color, you can find a successful artwork that goes against that rule or theory.

I must confess that I do most of my color choices in quilts and appliqué intuitively. From my vast collection of fabrics I will pull dozens of fabrics that I think will work. I then play around, shuffle, and rearrange them until I come up with the fabrics and color choices I think will best suit the project.

Aubry 1: I created this portrait of Aubry from the pattern that is included in my first book, *Faces and Places*. It looks all right, but I decided I could do better.

Aubry 2: I did a second version of Aubry, adding one more pattern line to the forehead. This meant I would need one more value of flesh color. The skin tones in this redone version are a definite improvement.

Real or Way Out

While painters may be able to achieve photo-realism with brush, canvas, and paint, it is physically impossible to do with fabric appliqué. What I hope to accomplish when I decide to attempt a realistic depiction is a simulation of reality—one that from a short distance appears shaded and dimensional, and that from a foot away will have the viewer awed by the great workmanship and intricate stitching when it is quite apparent close-up that the work is only swatches of fabric sewn together. So when I say "real" I mean relatively real or simply representative of something in reality.

In my experience, realistic colorations are among the most difficult to duplicate, and flesh tones are among the hardest to portray. First, because it's hard to combine just the right variations of tone and value, and second, because there just aren't as many flesh-toned fabrics available as we need. I feel fortunate that I have a fabulous quilt store near me. The ladies who work at Quilts, Etc., in Sandy, Utah, tell me they have 10,000 bolts of fabric, and I believe them. They have an extensive collection of solid-colored fabric. But even with the range of fabrics they have, I can barely put together five to seven shades of the flesh-tones I need.

Many times when I ask students to bring flesh-toned fabrics to class, if they are portraying a Caucasian person they come with these peachy-pink or salmony-coral colors. While you may think of these as being flesh-tones, and the top of the bolt may call the color "flesh," these fabrics are actually quite off the mark. And choosing fabric isn't any easier for dark-skinned people. Tans and browns are not popular colors right now. When shopping for flesh-tone fabric, hold your hand up to the bolt. You need to look for something close to the color of your hand. You probably won't find something that's an exact match, but possibly you can find something close to your own flesh tone. Start with that color and work from there. Choose one or two values that are lighter than that color you picked, and three or four colors that are progressively darker—from these you will have a shade run.

While I am discussing actual flesh colors and the skin tones of different races, I would like to say that, generally, the difference between the fabrics used for a light-skinned person as opposed to a dark-skinned person is not that much. Oftentimes, if one or two of the lightest values are dropped from a shade run used for a light-skinned person, and one or two dark values are added to that same shade run for a dark-skinned person, the shade run will work either way. I put together several values of tan to do Bob Melson's face (page 21). I have selected the fabrics to make Rohana Liyanage's portrait (see picture page 19) from my collection, and several of the fabrics I used for Bob are in the stack I'll be using for Rohanna. Bob is a cowboy from Montana, and Rohana is a post-doctorate student from Sri Lanka.

After I have chosen a possible shade run, I stack the fabrics in order of their value so all the folds of each fabric stagger an inch or two back from the last one. Then I stand three or four feet back and take a look to see if I can notice a definite difference among the fabrics. If they are visually too close in value, you won't be able to see a separation between each shape, and the work of sewing those shapes together will have gone for naught. I usually squint at the fabrics to see if there are "value steps" rather than blending. You could also use binoculars, turned to the wrong end, to accomplish the same thing.

Available among quilting notions are red and/or green clear plastic viewers. The purpose of these viewers is to determine the value of fabrics. I find I can do a better job of ascertaining shade differences by simply standing back and squinting.

LIGHTING FOR A FINISHED PIECE

You may also want to check out how your fabrics look under different lights. My sewing room has color-corrected flourescent light fixtures with bulbs that are supposed to emit a light that is closer to daylight than regular flourescent bulbs. I picked out all of the flesh tones for Bob Melson's face under these lights. After I stitched the portrait together, I thought it worked out quite well. In fact, when I had him mostly together, and before I stitched him to the background fabric, I hung him up on my sewing-room wall. Scruffy, my dog, came downstairs to check what I was doing, spotted Bob on the wall, and started barking at him and jumping up on the wall trying to get him. He thought we had a stranger in the house. So I knew my portrait of Bob looked good. I have hung the piece in my classrooms to show my students. Usually these rooms have flourescent lights as well, and Bob looked good there too.

Last month I was teaching in a room that had incandescent lights, and Bob looked different; the colors in his face weren't the same ones I had picked. Then, as I was doing photographs for the book and shooting under tungsten lights, I had the same problem. Some of the fabrics look grayed and some look a bit too red. I took the appliqué out into the daylight where it appeared closer to what it looked like in my sewing room, but still not quite as true to what I thought I had picked. The colors were still better than under the tungsten lights, anyhow.

So, if you have a particular location in mind for the quilt you are making, it's a good idea to check out your fabrics at that location. Or, if that's not possible, check them out in the type of lighting that is installed at that location in order to avoid unpleasant surprises.

> "The colors I use often describe the feeling of the scene rather than the actual reality because it is the tonal value and mood that is the essential information I need to retain. Any color that has the right value will work, despite it's unreality."
> Jane Corsellis, *Painting Figures in Light*

selected other than life-like color. You need to be able to look at a color and tell if it is a light, middle, or dark value, with steps in between each, and then plug those values into the proper places. You can't use pure purple for a shape you want to be light in value because it is a dark color. But you can use lavender, which is a tint of purple (tints are colors with white added to them) and very light in value. Here the red and/or green viewers may come in handy because they remove the color from fabrics when you use them. They also make values become more apparent.

In using non-real colors, you may want to consider the mood you want to create. Different colors create varying emotional effects because they have diverse associations. People tend to associate red with anger and heat. Blue can be calm and placid, but it can also seem cold and frigid. Using pure, multiple colors lends a carnival-like attitude.

Unreal

It is not necessary to pick colors you think are as close to reality as possible. Sometimes colors that are slightly off can be kind of charming. Then again, you can choose colors that are totally unlifelike. I recently visited the Wildlife of the American West Museum in Jackson, Wyoming. Almost all the paintings there strive for a sense of reality, and many acheive it. But my favorite painting among those that were on view was one of a bison that had been painted in pure, saturated primary and secondary colors. It was totally unnatural, but still recognizable, vibrant, and compelling.

Value is the key to making a subject or figure look shaded and dimensional, even if you have

SCANNING—COMPUTER HELP

Now, I know most computer graphics programs allow you to scan the picture itself and "posterize" it. This process reduces the value gradations in the photograph to a specified number of values. This works best on photographs that have wide-ranging values, and is much like what I do when I project images and trace them. But because there are so many variables in a picture, the shapes the computer configures tend to be very ragged. In this case, if you wanted to use the posterization command, you would scan the photograph, posterize it, print it, and then use tracing paper over the top of it to draw smooth lines. I find it is easier and faster to project the image and trace it rather than to do all the steps involved with having the computer convert it for me. However, it may be different for you.

I do make use of my computer graphics program in other ways. Sometimes, when I'm unsatisfied with the color choices I have made for portraits, I stitch the portrait again to see if I can do better. This presents a fairly heavy time investment since I mostly appliqué by hand. So one of my more worthwhile purchases this year was a scanner to go with my computer. Now, after I create a line drawing, I can scan that drawing into my computer and use my graphics program to play around with the color options.

All sorts of graphics/drawing programs and image editing programs are available. If you don't have one or are considering changing programs, you may want to consult *The Quilter's Computer Companion* by Judy Heim and Gloria Hansen. This book gives great advice on buying computer equipment and programs, and then letting those purchases aid in multitudes of creative quilting processes.

My image processing program, Aldus® Photo-Styler®, came with the purchase of my computer. So far, I have found it does almost everything my daughter Aubry (who does all sorts of graphics on the computer) and myself want it to.

I still consider myself relatively computer illiterate, so I'll briefly describe what I do with my drawings. (Every program is different, so I don't think it would be worthwhile to give you the exact commands I use.) First of all, I make sure that my drawing is traced in solid, black lines, and that all shapes are completely closed. If I have left the slightest gap in a line around a shape, the color I want to fill into that shape spills into the shape next to it and fills it up, as well. I scan the drawing I have made using the appropriate commands. It's helpful if the drawing is sized so it will fit onto the scanner bed. If not, kinko's copy store has oversize document copiers that will reduce large drawings to a workable size, which you can then scan. Once it is properly sized and all the settings are in place, I call up the program's color palette. This palette shows a box of blurred colors that I can choose by clicking on the mouse. A smaller box tells me which color I've selected. The high value colors tend to be at the bottom and the low value colors at the top, with an endless range of values in between. For a more specific choice, I can select an indexed-color image from the

color table, which shows each individual color in various gradations in its own box.

The PhotoStyler program has 16.7 million different colors. I've noticed computer software ads that brag their products have over one billion colors. However, between the eye and the brain, a human can only perceive about 32,000 color distinctions, so I think I am well covered in that department. My program will also do 256 shades of gray if I set it on grayscale. I've only been able to amass 50, if that many, of different solid gray, cotton fabrics after collecting them for over 12 years.

PhotoStyler has a bucket icon for the fill tool. I click on the bucket, click on the color I desire, and then click all the shapes on my drawing that I want to fill with that color. So, if I've numbered certain shapes as being color number one, I fill all those shapes with the selected color, usually chosen from the bottom area of the color palette because one is usually my lightest value. Then I move up the palette and choose a slightly darker value to fill my number two shapes, and so on. If I don't care for a color I've

Gumpy

chosen, it's very easy to change. I just select another color, click in the shape, and it's changed to that color. Playing with the PhotoStyler program this way, I can take my drawings and apply any sort of color scheme.

I took a photograph of my son's friend, Tommy "Gumpy" Montgomery, drew a line drawing from the projected photograph, and then colored the drawing several different ways using PhotoStyler. Here are some of the color options I came up with using the computer and scanner.

FUSE A FACE OR FIGURE

If you don't own a computer and a scanner (and maybe you have no desire to get one) you can still "try out" the fabrics you have chosen. You can make a fused mock-up of your drawing. Make sure you have solid, black lines on your pattern drawing. If you don't want to make a full-sized mock-up of your design, reduce it on a copy machine to a size where all the shapes are still of a size you can handle. Flip the pattern over and put it on a lightbox so you have a mirror-image. Put a paper-backed fusible material, such as WonderUnder, on top of the pattern and

Line Drawing Gumpy

Gray Scale Gumpy

Complementary Gumpy

Tricolor Gumpy

Purple Gumpy

This image does not work dimensionally. Colors added with no thought to value or shading.

Self-Portrait in Checkerboard, 1996, 15½" x 19¾", Margaret Cusack, Brooklyn, New York (photo by Gamma One Conversions). Taking off from a photo by Bonnie Ietaka, Margaret created this portrait of herself and comments, "I've always wanted to work with checkerboard fabrics and use them as value." The idea of doing four portraits in one was borrowed from Andy Warhol.

trace all the number one shapes onto a section, then all the number two shapes onto a section, and so on until you have all the shapes marked and sectioned according to the fabric they'll be fused to. Then fuse each section to the appropriate fabric.

Draw the entire pattern on the background fabric or the fabric you intend to fuse these shapes to. This will give you placement for each of the shapes. If you are only making this to try out your colors, simply cut the shapes, and don't worry about them meeting perfectly or about the order you fuse them to the background. If, however, you want it to look good or it to be useable, you'll want to be very careful about the cutting and placement of the shapes.

Fuse larger shapes in the order that those shapes appear. In actuality a shape that is on the side of a face would go under a shape that is on the front of a face. A recessed eye-socket goes behind the brow ridge and cheek, so the shapes that are behind would be fused first. You may want to consider cutting an "underlap" or slight allowance beyond the edge of a shape that goes under another piece, so that there will be no gaps between shapes. Tiny shapes like parts of the eye or lips are easier to fuse on top of larger shapes. Hair, glasses, clothing, etc., go on top of flesh parts.

After you have created this fused picture, you may decide you are finished. You do not need to make a sewn version of it. This is perfectly acceptable if all you want is a wallhanging. Margaret Cusack has made some wonderful portraits using only fabric and fusibles.

Bill Clinton, 1996, 11¾" x 14", Margaret Cusack, Brooklyn, New York (photo by Gamma One Conversions). This portrait takes its inspiration from several photos. Margaret feels that Clinton can be a rather dynamic, modern figure. The construction only involves cut fabric fused in place with WonderUnder.

Take your fused work, stretch it, mat it, and/or frame it. It will look terrific. If you have something more durable in mind, you may want to use the sewing machine to go over the edges with satin stitching. Using fusibles makes the finished product rather stiff, though. In the next chapter I will demonstrate how the pieces of a portrait can be put together using only a fusible thread and afterward covering the raw edges with satin stitch. This makes for a very soft, light, and flexible product, much like the weight a hand appliqué project would be.

"When you get right down to it, a rainbow isn't located at a specific place in space, it's located in the space behind your eyes, in that lump of tissue called your brain."—Pat Murphy & Paul Doherty in their article, "Watch the Skies," December 1997, *Fantasy & Science Fiction Magazine.*

Tina Turner, 1997, 18" x 28", Margaret Cusack, Brooklyn, New York (photo by Gamma One Conversions). Margaret has been working in a new style using checkerboard fabrics. Working from several photos to establish her drawing, she wanted to create a portrait of Tina Turner because she felt Tina would be a good subject for this new style. As she says, "Tina's personality is energetic, colorful, and electric, and that's how I feel about this new work."

CHAPTER EIGHT

Working Through Projects

"I hear and I forget. I see and I remember. I do and I understand."
—Chinese proverb

MAPPING A ROUTE

Once you have completed drawing your pattern, having gone over the lines with a fine black marker, selected the fabrics in the colors, values, and shades you are going to use, it is time to start sewing your project. For most projects, the subject is broken up into workable sections which usually contain a certain set of shades and values of a selected color. (Details within that section can be of other colors.)

Briefly reviewing the process, there are exceptions, but most of the time you will want to start with the lightest shade of the fabric, drawing all lines from the section on to that fabric using a lightbox. A blank piece of the second lightest fabric is then pinned underneath. Only the shapes that are labeled number one are going to be kept from that top layer of fabric. This means that you can cut anywhere in the top layer of fabric that is not labeled as being a number one shape. Cutting may seem very intimidating to you. After all, once a cut is made in fabric it cannot be put back together. Seam allowances need to be carefully planned and thought out before you actually start cutting.

There is a method for you to plan ahead and diagram just where you are going to start your stitching and cutting for each layer. It is essentially what you do when you plan an extended road trip and you are using a road map—you take a marker and highlight the route you intend to drive.

You will need your pattern, several sheets of tracing paper, and two colors of some kind of marking implement. (You may have to erase, so consider something that can be removed or erased from tracing paper.) Designate one color for signifying your stitching lines and the other color as indicating your cutting lines. The colors are not important, just make sure they are different enough to readily tell one from the other. For example: red lines can equal stitching lines, green lines can equal cutting lines.

Place the tracing paper over the section of the pattern you have chosen to work on. Look for lines that have a shape labeled number one on one side and have a shape labeled number two on the other side. In other words, these two shapes share a common line. These are your stitching lines for the first layer. With your red marker, trace all the lines that number one and number two shapes have in common. Look over your pattern carefully to make sure you have found every line that qualifies. Now comes the decision-making part.

With your green marker you are going to designate your cutting lines. Remember, only the number one shapes are going to be kept from that top layer of fabric. So the seamlines need to be cut around the number one shapes, but not necessarily all the way around the shapes. Draw your green cutting lines a seam allowance's distance away from the red lines you have marked, tapering where it is called for, such as into corners, on the opposite side of the lines that make up the number one shapes. Your cutting lines can be drawn anywhere that is not labeled number one but you need to be restrictive in just how much cutting you plan to do. Of course you need to have cutting lines for seam allowances, but you also need to cut away excess fabric that will be in the way when you proceed to the next layer. Number two shapes need to be redrawn on the number two fabric, so if after seamlines are cut, there is still number one fabric on top of the number two shapes, it needs to be removed. But you don't want to cut away too much too soon. Draw cutting lines that will keep the maximum amount of the number one fabric but still remove any that is in the way. Using a dotted line, draw basting lines that will hold fabrics together where you need to cut away fabric but there isn't any stitching to hold the pieces together. (Basting will keep gaping holes from forming in the work and keep the integrity of the piece.)

Once you have what you think are all the stitching and cutting lines marked on your first layer of

Gumpy Route Maps

tracing paper, look at it for several moments. Study it carefully. Picture in your mind what will be the consequences of cutting in the places you have marked. Will you be cutting away something you need; or, are you getting rid of enough number one fabric or too much? Once you have decided your map works, you can transfer those cutting lines to your actual fabric, if you want. Go ahead and stitch that layer in the manner you have laid out on your tracing paper.

After completing that layer, make a map for the second layer. Trace with your designated color marker all the seamlines where the number one and two shapes adjoin the number three shapes . Then figure out what the cutting lines will be. When deciding on these cutting lines, you also need to consider cuts that were made on the layer before. Study this map and if it looks right, go ahead and stitch that layer.

You can make a map for every layer you plan to stitch. If you take all these tracing paper maps and lay them one over the other, carefully aligning the pattern, all the lines that make up the pattern will have been traced except for the ones that make up the outside edges of the figure or form. Here are examples of "maps" of the first three layers of the face section for Gumpy's portrait from page 66.

The idea came from the step-by-step projects, in *Faces & Places,* which feature different lines from the pattern that are highlighted with red to designate stitching lines and green to represent cutting lines.

SWEATING THE DETAILS—BOB MELSON

I do not advocate going into great detail on every little thing for every portrait. Creating detail can be tedious. But I do think a certain amount is needed to add interest to a fabric portrait. Pick and choose your details because those little things can bring something to life.

Bob Melson's portrait is one of the more detailed ones I have done. I thought that maybe pointing out some of the details might inspire you to figure out ways of accomplishing details in your own projects.

For starters, let's look at some of his clothing. Without shading and wrinkles added, clothing looks flat and paperdoll-like. Bob's shirt is plaid (one naturally thinks of cowboys as wearing plaid). Working off my values theory, I decided I would use three different plaid fabrics, each containing approximately the same hues but with light, medium, and dark values. I stitched the yoke and collar of his shirt together using these three plaids, but when I stood back and looked at what I had put together, it did not

Wrong plaid for Bob's shirt

Good plaid for Bob's shirt

work. The plaids did not blend together to make the shirt look like one entity. Instead, it looked like a shirt with contrasting collar and yoke and the darkest plaid didn't look like anything at all.

So I started over. This time I selected a plaid that was fairly basic and then chose fabrics with a slight bit of texture that were a medium and dark value of the basic blue of my chosen plaid. This combination works and looks like the shadows and draping of his shirt even though the two darker values do not have a hint of plaid in them.

All parts of Bob were constructed independent of the background and assembled together except for the ties of his hat and parts of his sunglasses. Both of these things required the background to be present before I could stitch them on.

One lens of Bob's sunglasses could be made before doing the background. In this lens you can see his eye behind the glass. To do this, I constructed a separate eye, much like the eye project (page 40), then put black organza over the top of this swatch. I cut the organza to the shape of the lens, plus seam allowances, and stitched it in place. The other lens is actually more complicated, so I'll show you the steps of that one in a moment.

Background for Bob

I then put together my background. This I did with machine blind-stitch appliqué and satin stitch appliqué. Notice that I left the area were Bob is to be appliquéd mostly blank (no sense doing any sort of work there when it's going to be covered up and cut away).

Bob on background with one hat string

I stitched Bob to the background, leaving an opening under his mustache so I could slip the end of his hat string under it. I have also left an opening in his hat over his right ear for the other string. After he was stitched in place, the excess background fabric was cut away from behind him so I don't have a build-up of layers. Then I stitched down that first hat string. (All by itself it kind of makes him look like he's drooling or something, doesn't it?)

Bob mostly done

DETAIL 1

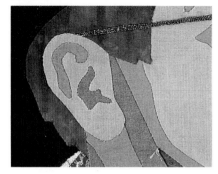

Embroidered ear piece

Bob's right ear piece for his sunglasses is under the hat string so I have to embroider that first. After that I can complete the hat strings with the slide.

DETAIL 2

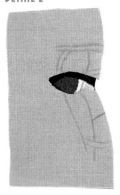

Now it is time to make the other sunglass lens. I had to wait to do this one because the background shows through the lens and I needed to see where everything was going to be placed. I made a tracing of the eye, the edge of the hat, and the sunglasses frame from the pattern, then placed it over the actual appliqué to see where the seams in the background landed. Then I traced those lines. Now I could begin to construct this part.

I began with the section of his face with the eye in it and stitched it together.

DETAIL 3

This face section was then stitched to a piece of the hat fabric where the shapes from those parts adjoined. The lines for the hat, background, and sunglasses frame were then redrawn on the hat fabric.

DETAIL 4

I then joined the three background fabrics together in strips of the required width, put this section behind the hat and face, stitched where these fabrics joined, and redrew the lines of the frame on the background fabrics.

DETAIL 5

The left ear piece can be seen through the lens of the sunglasses. This needed to be embroidered in the proper place on top of the hat fabric.

DETAIL 6

All the elements contained within the lens are now present.

To achieve the look of sunglasses, black silk organza is placed over the lens construct and basted in place just outside the seamline. I try to create a "bubble" over the construct with the organza, so that when the seam allowances are turned under there will be some ease and the fabrics under the organza will not pucker. This lens shape is then trimmed with a seam allowance.

DETAIL 7

The lens is carefully stitched in place, making sure that the face, hat, and background edges are aligned. Where the lens adjoins the nose, the layering has to be reversed, which is why the seam on the bridge of his nose was only basted in place. (See basting on nose on page 73.)

DETAIL 8

In this photograph the basting of the nose has been removed and the remaining edge of the lens tucked underneath it.

In this next photograph, the bridge of the nose has been carefully stitched in place and the left lens is complete. Because I went to the trouble of doing these layers like I did, the lens looks like a lens and no raw edges of the organza are visible.

The last step completing his portrait is to embroider the lens frames in place, which I did with a different metallic thread than the one I used for the ear pieces.

I can't report how many hours Bob's portrait has taken me to make because I haven't kept track of the time. However, the glasses including both lenses took about five hours and I believe the work was certainly worth it for the look I achieved. Here is a quote that I think is applicable:

"Genius is nothing but a greater aptitude for patience."

—*George de Buffon*

Bob's completed portrait

The Wrangler, 1998, 41" x 36", Charlotte Warr Andersen, Salt Lake City, Utah, (photo by Thomas Anastasion).

PORTRAIT BY MACHINE—CARLEEN

For those of you with a bit less patience, I have come up with a method for doing the reverse layering process on the sewing machine. If you don't mind using fusible to back every piece of fabric, building up layer upon layer which results in a very stiff piece, then go for it. But if you would like a finished piece that is light and flexible you may want to try this method.

If you wish to do the following project you will need: a sewing machine in good working order that can make a cover (satin) stitch, Threadfuse® (a thread that looks like dental floss, but is an iron-on bonding agent), four shades or values of flesh-tone fabric, two lip-color fabrics, a swatch of white fabric, three shades or values of hair fabric, four different fabrics for the clothing, a background fabric, thread to match all of the fabrics as closely as possible (machine embroi-dery thread is preferred), a lightbox, iron and ironing board, and Sulky® Totally Stable iron-on stabilizer. The Threadfuse is to be used in the bobbin of the machine. You should use a thread to match your fabric on the upper sewing machine thread.

In the step-by-step pictures that follow, I will be using a bright-colored contrasting thread so that you can see the stitching. This created minor problems for me when I did the cover stitching, so I don't advise doing it on an actual project.

I drew a relatively simple pattern from the photograph of my niece, Carleen, then went over it with a fine, black marker.

The portrait is to be worked in sections: face, hair, and clothing. I put the pattern on the lightbox with the lightest flesh tone on top of it and traced all the lines of the face onto it using a removable marker. I also drew small portions of the lines of other sections to show intersecting points.

Carleen in profile

For workability, enlarge pattern 130% for Carleen.

1-4	**Flesh tones**
L1-L2	**Lips**
J1-J2	**Jacket**
T1-T2	**Turtleneck**
H1-H3	**Hair**

FACE 1

Using a pink marker, I have traced over the line I am going to be stitching. (This pink line is on the opposite side of the line than it would be if I were hand appliquéing.) The stitching line goes on top of the edge of the shapes I am going to keep out of this layer where they adjoin the next layer. In this case, the stitching line will be just inside the number one shapes where they adjoin the number two shapes.

FACE 2

Stitch ¹⁄₁₆" inside the line, starting and stopping exactly where number one no longer touches number two. There is no need to backstitch. Carefully cut both the upper and lower threads next to the stitching. I have done this stitching with red thread.

FACE 3

On the wrong side of the piece you can see the Threadfuse.

FACE 4

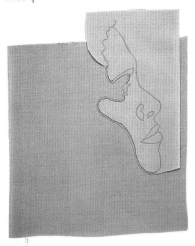

Lay this piece on top of the second lightest flesh-tone, take it to the ironing board, and fuse the two pieces by pressing over the stitching. (Note: nothing is drawn on this second piece of fabric, yet.) Make sure your iron is hot enough to melt the Threadfuse but not so hot it will make it vanish completely or scorch your fabric. You may want to do a few test pieces first. Check that the fusing is relatively secure. This is not enough fusing to make it a permanent bond; think of it as only being temporary until the cover stitching is done. The fusing is somewhat delicate so don't use too much force when handling these fused pieces. Take some small, sharp scissors and cut as close to the stitching as possible. You should be cutting along the line drawn for the number one shape. Cut across any gaps between stitching so that you are cutting away the excess number one fabric, such as the middle of the eyebrow.

FACE 5

Return the piece to the lightbox, and carefully align the existing shapes with the pattern. Redraw any of the lines that are missing.

FACE 6

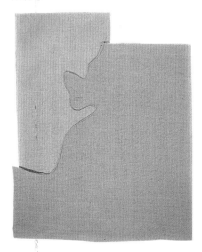

Flip the piece over to the wrong side on the lightbox — you can see where the fabrics overlap. Draw a line that shows the fabrics overlapping $\frac{3}{16}$". This is your cutting line for the number two fabric. Carefully cut away the number two fabric and the piece will be back to one layer, except where the fabrics that have a $\frac{3}{16}$" overlap.

FACE 7

The next step is to stitch everywhere that the number one and two shapes adjoin the number three fabric. On this particular pattern only the number two shapes touch the number three shapes. I have done the stitching with blue thread for this layer.

FACE 8

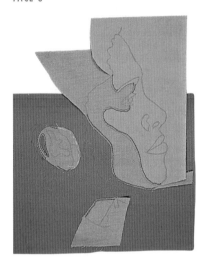

Lay this piece on top of the number three fabric and fuse it. Notice the line of white hand-basting that holds the ear in place so that excess fabric can be cut away.

Carefully trim away the excess number two fabric, revealing the number three fabric underneath.

FACE 9

Return to the lightbox, and redraw the missing lines on the number three fabric.

FACE 10

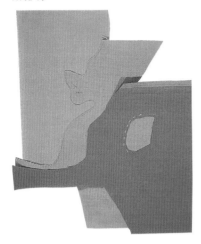

Flip the piece over on the lightbox and draw ³⁄₁₆" overlap. Cut along this line to remove the excess number three fabric.

FACE 11

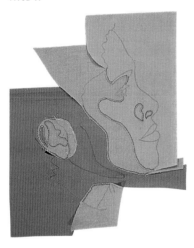

Stitch everywhere that number one, two, and three shapes adjoin number four shapes. I have used green thread for this layer of stitching.

FACE 12

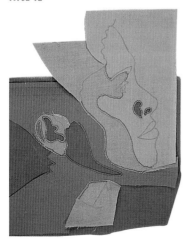

Fuse to a piece of the number four flesh-tone. Carefully trim away excess number one, two and three fabrics from next to the stitching, revealing the number four fabric in the appropriate shapes. Return to the lightbox and redraw any missing lines.

FACE 13

Flip the piece over on the lightbox and draw the $^3/_{16}$" overlap. Trim away the excess number four fabric.

LIPS 1

Next put the lips in place one at a time. Do the upper lip first stitch along the top line of the upper lip; I've done it with yellow thread. Notice that even though I am stitching on the number one fabric, I am doing the stitching in the lip shape. This is because I intend to do my cover stitch with lip-colored thread. Place a piece of the upper lip fabric behind the work and fuse in place. Notice the white hand-basting in the lower lip to hold the lips together after I've cut away the fabric.

LIPS 2

A wedge of the number one fabric is cut away to reveal the lip fabric. The piece is returned to the lightbox and the missing lip lines are redrawn.

LIPS 3

Flip the piece to the wrong side and trim away any excess lip fabric.

LIPS 4

Stitch the bottom line of the upper and lower lip, shown here in yellow thread.

LIPS 5

Fuse a swatch of the lower lip fabric behind the piece. Cut away the excess number one and upper lip fabrics to reveal the lower lip. Trim away the excess lower lip fabric from behind.

EYES 1

Redraw the missing line of the lower lip. Stitch around the shape of the eye as shown in yellow thread. The iris and eyelashes will be done with appropriately colored threads so the only fabric that needs to be incorporated is the eye white.

EYES 2

Fuse the swatch of white fabric behind. Trim number one fabric from on top to reveal the white, then redraw the missing lines for the eye, and trim away the excess white fabric from behind the piece. Make the eyebrow in the same manner as the eye white.

EYES 3

The face section is now complete. The wrong side of the work looks like this.

HAIR 1

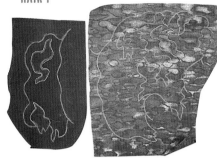

Set the face section aside and work on the hair. The hair is divided into two sections: the crown of the head and the ponytail. Stitch around the shapes in the crown where the number one fabric meets the number two fabric and in the ponytail where the number three fabric meets the number two fabric.

HAIR 2

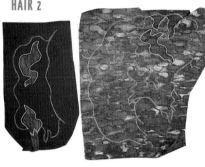

Fuse the number two fabric behind the crown and ponytail. Trim away top fabrics revealing the number two shapes. Trim excess number two fabric from behind the pieces and redraw any missing lines.

HAIR 3

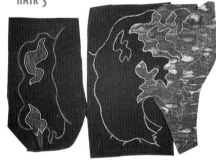

Stitch along lines in the crown where the number one shapes adjoin the number three shapes. Fuse to fabric number three and trim excess number one fabric from the top and excess number three fabric from the back. Redraw any missing lines.

HAIR 4

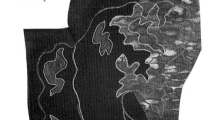

Stitch around the remaining number two shape in the crown of the head and where the crown adjoins the ponytail. Fuse small swatch of number two fabric behind the shape, being careful not to fuse line for ponytail. Trim excess number three fabric from on top to reveal number two shape and trim excess number two fabric from behind. Trim next to stitching at the back of the crown where the ponytail attaches before the fusing is done so you can see where lines meet. Fuse the ponytail in place.

HAIR 5

Stitch the hair section along the hairline where it touches the face, ear, and neck. This stitching is done with purple thread in my sample. Trim away excess fabric from along this line before fusing. Carefully place the hair on top of the face and fuse in place. Trim the excess flesh tones away from under the hair.

SHIRT 1

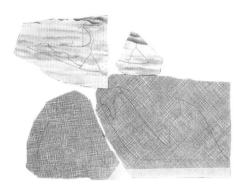

The clothing is next. I actually used two different parts of the same fabric for the light and dark shapes of the turtleneck to give a good shadow effect. Draw sections and stitch where T-1 adjoins T-2 and J-1 adjoins J-2 as shown.

SHIRT 2

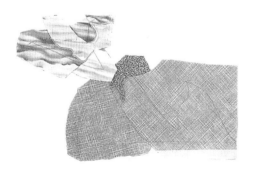

Fuse fabrics T-2 and J-2 in place, trim away excess T-1 and J-1 fabrics from the top and excess T-2 and J-2 from the back. Redraw any missing lines. Stitch along where collar of turtleneck overlaps small triangle section of T-1, fuse in place, and trim away excess fabrics. Stitch along where collar of jacket overlaps the shoulder and fuse in place on top of shoulder section. Sections should look like this.

SHIRT 3

Stitch along the neckline of the jacket. Trim next to this stitching before fusing. Align the jacket carefully on top of the turtleneck and fuse in place. Trim away excess turtleneck fabric from behind.

SHIRT 4

Stitch along the neckline of the turtleneck and the collar of the jacket where they overlap the neck and hair. Trim next to this stitching before fusing. Carefully align the clothing on top of the neck and hair and fuse in place. Trim excess neck and hair fabrics from behind the piece.

SHIRT 5

All fabrics are now in place for the portrait and this figure needs to be applied to a background. Stitch around all the outside edges of the figure except for the bottom of the portrait. I have done my stitching in red thread — you should match your thread to the fabric as you work around the figure. Trim all the excess fabric from around the figure cutting close to the stitching. If any edges of the figure cup or curl under because the thread tension is a little off, clip the thread where needed but try not to do it too much. Look to see if your fabric is laying flat as you are doing the stitching to avoid this problem. The figure should look like this.

SHIRT 6

The back side of the work looks like this.

Fuse the figure to the background.

Trim away the excess background fabric from behind the figure. The back side should look like this.

Gently go over the piece with an iron to make sure the bonds are holding and the piece is flat. Fuse a piece of Sulky Totally Stable stabilizer big enough to cover all the areas that are to be stitched to the back side of the work. Now the cover (satin) stitching will be done. Match your thread as closely as possible to the fabric. Matching can be a problem because, as with fabrics, there just aren't that many flesh-colored threads available. Do the best you can. The thread can actually match the fabric on either side of the cover stitch in certain cases; you just need to decide which fabric needs to be matched.

Start with areas where both ends of the stitching will go under the rows of stitching that will follow. For example: the line of her profile on one end goes under her hair and one goes under her lip. You can also stitch shapes that are complete in themselves, such as her nostril and nose flare.

LIPS 1

For her lips, I decided on two different colors. I do the bottom lip first because the ends of the stitching for it go under stitching to follow. Also notice that I have stitched the iris adjusting my stitch width as I sewed to achieve an oval shape.

LIPS 2

The remaining lip edges are covered with the stitching for the upper lip. I taper my stitch width to make the corner of her lips pointed. I have also completed the eye by stitching the eyelashes in two colors with appropriately tapering stitch-widths.

FIGURE 1

After covering all raw edges with a cover stitch, my portrait of Carleen is complete.

FIGURE 2

I tear away the stabilizer from the back of the work and the piece is lightweight but sturdy. The back looks like this.

Ryan portrait

I make no claims to being a machine whiz. My specialties are hand appliqué and precision piecing. But my portrait of Carleen turned out relatively well. I could not match the threads as closely as I would have liked and I find the ridge of the cover stitch a bit distracting. But on the plus side, the project took me about eight to ten hours (and that includes me photographing every step) and would have taken me two to three times longer to do by hand.

I have done another machine portrait of my nephew, Ryan. The line drawing for him is on page 10 and this is the way his portrait by machine turned out. I made one mistake on him. I had neglected to label the shape of his right eyelid according to what shade it was going to be. I assumed without thinking that it was a number one shape when it should have been a number two shape. His eyebrow sticks out most unnaturally.

Margaret Cusack is an artist from Brooklyn, New York who is exceedingly competent with a sewing machine. I believe her machine is an actual extension of her mind and hands. Her stitched artwork was featured on the cover of the Dec. 8, 1997 cover of *Time* magazine. I scanned over the photo of her stitching on my copy of the magazine and could not find one flawed stitch and you can see every stitch in this photo. Margaret has done many wonderful commissions for private and corporate accounts including a Bill Gates voodoo doll for *Forbes* magazine. Three of her pieces are shown (page 93), as well as others interspersed inside this book. These portraits feature shaded fabric and cover stitch.

If I were as good with my machine as Margaret is, I might be doing more machine work.

Postscript

Once again, I feel as if I've emptied my brain on to the pages of this book. Instead of thinking that I've said all I have to say on the subject, I'll view this as an opportunity to fill my brain with more ideas and challenges.

This book is to be used as instruction and inspiration. Feel free to use the projects and drawings I've incorporated if you want to for your own purposes. However, my intent in writing this book is to give you the knowledge and impetus to try making fabric portraits of your own loved ones, or whoever else you would like.

It is learnable and doable, but it takes the right attitude. Negative thinking and saying I couldn't possibly do that!" will get you nowhere. If you don't at least try it you don't really know that you can't do it. If you are afraid of using up time on experimentation or cutting up fabric uselessly, I'd advise you to loosen up. Mistakes are nothing to be afraid of, view them as learning opportunities instead. The only people who never make mistakes are those who do nothing.

I have three more words of advice for you — GO FOR IT!

Schuyler's First Fish, 1997, 34" x 50", Joanne Traise, Omaha, Nebraska (photo by Thomas Anastasion). Based on a photograph taken when Joanne's grandson was five, which she treasured for the look of pride on his face. That look has come across well in the fabric. The traditional pieced background is a fun addition.

Bishop Mugavero, 1994, 35" x 43", Margaret Cusack, Brooklyn, New York (photo by Ron Breland). This sensitive portrait of Bishop Mugavero is part of "A Time for Hope", the huge hanging seen on this page. It is machine appliquéd using damask, cotton and satin fabrics.

Barbara Gordon, 1972, 18" x 24", Margaret Cusack, Brooklyn, New York (photo by Margaret Cusack). This is one of Cusack's earlier portraits. Margaret writes, " I was establishing myself as an illustrator using stitched artwork as my medium. Barbara Gordon was my agent from 1972 - 78 and I felt that a portrait of her would show potential clients that I could capture her likeness."

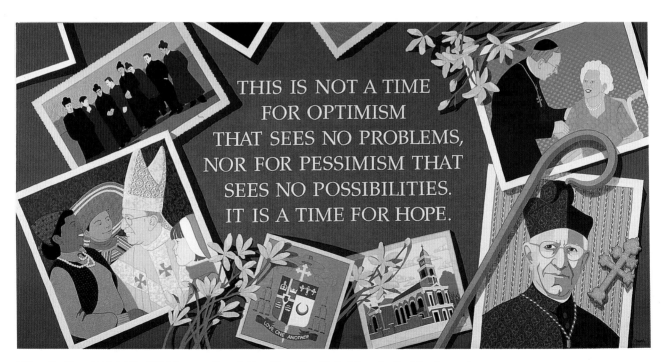

A Time For Hope, 1994, 144" x 72", Margaret Cusack, Brooklyn, New York, (photo by Paul Armbruster). This mural size wallhanging was commissioned for a nursing home in Brooklyn.

SOURCE LIST

Tracer and other opaque projectors:
Artograph, 2838 Vicksburg Lane, N.
Plymouth, Minnesota 55447
(800) 328-4653

Alpha Numeric Paper:
Beaver Paper and Packaging, Norcross, Georgia
(800) 768-2700

Threadfuse:
Available at many quilt and fabric stores including
JoAnn's Fabrics.

DMC Machine Embroidery Thread as well as many
other brands and kinds of threads:
Creative Stitches (Wholesale and Retail)
230 West 1700 South
Salt Lake City, Utah 84115
(800) 748-5144

Lightboxes:
Staples Office Supplies
Phone 1-800-378-2753 for customer service and store
locations.

For quilting supplies:
Cotton Patch Mail Order
3405 Hall Lane, Dept. CTB, Lafayette, CA 94549
e-mail: cottonpa@aol.com
(800) 835-4418
(925) 283-7883

For more information, write for a free catalog to:
C&T Publishing, Inc.
P.O. Box 1456, Lafayette, CA 94549
(800) 284-1114
http://www.ctpub.com
e-mail: ctinfo@ctpub.com

BIBLIOGRAPHY

Andersen, Charlotte Warr, *Faces & Places - Images in Appliqué* (C&T Publishing, Lafayette, CA, 1995)

Boswell, Ron, *The Fundamentals of Photography* (Ron Boswell, Salt Lake City, 1996)

Corsellis, Jane, *Painting Figures in Light* (Watson-Guptill Publications, New York, 1982)

Gair, Angela, *Tonal Values - How to See Them, How to Paint Them* (North Light Books, Cincinatti, Ohio, 1987)

Heim, Judy & Hansen, Gloria, *The Quilter's Computer Companion* (No Starch Press, San Francisco, 1998)

Hogarth, Burne, *Drawing Dynamic Hands* (Watson-Guptill Publications, New York, 1977)

Hogarth, Burne, *Drawing the Human Head* (Watson-Guptill Publications, New York, 1965)

Jacobs, Ted Seth, *Light for the Artist* (Watson-Guptill Publications, New York, 1988)

Kent, Sarah, *Composition* (Dorling Kindersley Publishing, Inc., New York, 1995)

Lawrence, Margaret, *Hearts and Bones* (Avon Books, New York, 1997)

Pedoe, Dan, *Geometry and the Visual Arts* (Dover Publications, New York, 1976)

Wolfrom, Joen, *The Magical Effects of Color* (C&T Publishing, Lafayette, CA, 1992)

After being thoroughly immersed in many of the needle arts for her first three decades, quiltmaking and teaching the processes for making art quilts has become Charlotte's career of choice. As with most quilters, she started out making traditional quilts and soon came to realize the pictorial and representational possibilities inherent in the fabric medium. Though Charlotte includes a wide range of subject matter in her quilts her favorite topics for portrayal are people and the creation of faces is considered her specialty.

Charlotte's quilts are in the collections of several museums, such as the Museum of the American Quilters Society in Paducah, Kentucky and the Museum of American Folk Art in New York City, and are also held by many private collectors. She has won many awards for her quilts including two Best of Show awards at the Houston International Quilt Festival.

Traveling and teaching consumes much of Charlotte's time, with workshop and lecture venues located locally, nationally and internationally. The other main consumer of Charlotte's time is her family; Eskild, her husband, and four children, Amity, Dylan, Aubry, and Davyn, all still living at home, and two faithful dogs, Betsy and Scruffy. She fits her quiltmaking into the hours she can grab between teaching and family.

Charlotte is a native of Salt Lake City, Utah, where she has lived all her life. She is an avid reader of science fiction, horror and fantasy, loves alternative rock music, and enjoys watching old (pre-1960's) movies while sewing.

Charlotte's first book, *Faces & Places—Images in Appliqué,* may be purchased at your favorite quilt store or may be order through C&T Publishing.

If you are interested in Charlotte's workshops on drawing and creating faces and figures, or other classes and lectures, send an e-mail: andersen@burgoyne.com, or write to her at 5740 Wilderland Lane, Salt Lake City, Utah 84118.